DEVELOPMENT CENTRE STUDIES

A MANAGEMENT APPROACH TO PROJECT APPRAISAL AND EVALUATION

with special reference to non-directly productive projects

by

N. Imboden

DEVELOPMENT CENTRE
OF THE ORGANISATION
FOR ECONOMIC CO-OPERATION AND DEVELOPMENT

The Organisation for Economic Co-operation and Development (OECD) was set up under a Convention signed in Paris on 14th December 1960, which provides that the OECD shall promote policies designed:
— to achieve the highest sustainable economic growth and employment and a rising standard of living in Member countries, while maintaining financial stability, and thus to contribute to the development of the world economy;
— to contribute to sound economic expansion in Member as well as non-member countries in the process of economic development;
— to contribute to the expansion of world trade on a multilateral, non-discriminatory basis in accordance with international obligations.

The Members of OECD are Australia, Austria, Belgium, Canada, Denmark, Finland, France, the Federal Republic of Germany, Greece, Iceland, Ireland, Italy, Japan, Luxembourg, the Netherlands, New Zealand, Norway, Portugal, Spain, Sweden, Switzerland, Turkey, the United Kingdom and the United States.

The Development Centre of the Organisation for Economic Co-operation and Development was established by decision of the OECD Council on 23rd October 1962.

The purpose of the Centre is to bring together the knowledge and experience available in Member countries of both economic development and the formulation and execution of general policies of economic aid; to adapt such knowledge and experience to the actual needs of countries or regions in the process of development and to put the results at the disposal of the countries by appropriate means.

The Centre has a special and autonomous position within the OECD which enables it to enjoy scientific independence in the execution of its task. Nevertheless, the Centre can draw upon the experience and knowledge available in the OECD in the development field.

* *
*

The opinions expressed and arguments employed in this publication
are the responsibility of the author
and do not necessarily represent those of the OECD.

CONTENTS

Preface 7

Part I

PROJECT APPRAISAL METHODOLOGIES

I. INTRODUCTIONS AND DEFINITIONS 11

   1. Introduction 11
   2. Definitions 12
   3. A methodology for the appraisal of non-directly
       productive projects 17

II. PLANNING, PROJECT SELECTION, APPRAISAL
    AND EVALUATION 20

   1. Introduction 20
   2. Project appraisal/evaluation as part of a
       development management system 21
   3. The information needs of a project appraisal
       exercise 24
   4. Different types of project appraisal 26
   5. Difficulties of a project appraisal/evaluation
       exercise 28
   6. Desirable characteristics of a project appraisal
       methodology 30

III. PROJECT APPRAISAL METHODOLOGIES 33

   1. Social cost benefit analysis 33
   2. Cost-effectiveness analysis 38
   3. The Prou and Chervel Appraisal Method 38
   4. The impact approach to the appraisal of projects .. 41
   5. Project appraisal in reality 44

IV. SELECTED ANNOTATED REFERENCES 48

Part II

A MANAGEMENT APPROACH TO
DEVELOPMENT ACTIVITIES

I. INTRODUCTION 57

II. THE PROJECT CYCLE 59

III. SOCIAL INDICATORS AS ELEMENTS OF AN
INFORMATION SYSTEM 62

    1. The use of social indicators within a manage-
ment system for development activities 63
    2. The iterative systems approach to social
indicators 63
    3. Definition and characteristics of social
indicators 64
    4. Possible errors in social indicators 69
    5. A taxonomy of social indicators 70

IV. THE DIFFERENT LEVELS OF ANALYSIS 71

    1. The analysis of the social trajectory 71
    2. A first approximation of social objectives 73
    3. Goals analysis and operationalisation of goals ... 74
    4. Sectoral analysis 78
    5. The local level or micro-analysis 83
    6. The integration of the analyses and their
interdependence 88

V. PROJECT APPRAISAL WITHIN A MANAGEMENT
SYSTEM 89

    1. Determination of expected contributions of
alternative actions to the various goals 90
    2. The determination of costs and benefits of a
project 95
    3. Two practical problems 100

VI. RESUME AND CONCLUSIONS 103

VII. SELECTED ANNOTATED REFERENCES 106

4

Part III

SETTING UP A MONITORING EVALUATION/SYSTEM FOR SOCIAL PROGRAMMES

I.   INTRODUCTION 117

II. CURRENT REPORTING/EVALUATION PRACTICES ... 118

III. MAJOR PROBLEMS OF CURRENT MONITORING/
     EVALUATION EFFORTS 123

IV. TYPES OF EVALUATION 126

V.   SETTING UP A MONITORING/EVALUATION
     SYSTEM FOR A GOVERNMENT AGENCY 131

     1. Determination of the formation needs of a
         Government Agency 131
     2. Determination of who needs the information 132
     3. Determination of the degree of confidence needed .. 133
     4. The choice of an evaluation system 134

VI. SETTING UP A MONITORING/EVALUATION
     SYSTEM FOR A SPECIFIC PROGRAMME OR
     PROJECT 137

     1. What should be monitored/evaluated? 138
     2. What can be monitored/evaluated? 141
     3. The choice of a monitoring/evaluation design 146
     4. Data collection, processing and presentation 154

VII. INSTITUTIONAL ASPECTS OF MONITORING/
     EVALUATION 160

VIII. RESUME AND CONCLUSIONS 164

IX. SELECTED ANNOTATED REFERENCES 166

LIST OF FIGURES

I.   Management System for Development Activities 25
II. Project Appraisal in a Management System 27
III. The Logical Structure of the Impact Approach 42

5

IV.   Logical Framework Matrix   43

V.   The Project Cycle   60

VI.   Partial Specification of Goals, Objectives, Means
and Alternatives based on the Vth Plan of India   77

VII.   Means–Goals Interdependence: Goal Specification   79

VIII.   The Integration of Analyses and their Interdependence..   87

IX.   Health: Means - Ends Relationship   94

X.   Expected Contributions of Alternative Rice
Production Projects to Various Development Goals   96

XI.   Product Path Analysis   100

XII.   Types of Evaluation and Their Characteristics   130

XIII.   Setting up a Monitoring/Evaluation System for a
Government Agency   136

XIV.   A Project Performance Network Chart   144

XV.   Setting up a Monitoring/Evaluation System for a
Specific Programme or Project   147

XVI.   Data Collection Design and their Characteristics   153

XVII.   Policy Development and Evaluation Designs   155

PREFACE

This publication on project appraisal/evaluation is addressed to Government officials in less developed countries and aid agencies who are concerned with the management of development activities. The goal of the book is to provide the necessary information to development managers so that they can set up their own appraisal/evaluation framework in a technically competent way. The book is based on the premise that appraisal/evaluation frameworks have to be adapted to the socio-economic situation of a given country. Each country has its own development path, its specific goals and its own management structure and hence needs its own tailormade appraisal/evaluation framework. The "manual" approach is therefore rejected.

Rather than propose a specific and rigid framework, the book discusses the various concepts and frameworks proposed and attempts to highlight the factors that have to be taken into account when choosing and setting up an appraisal/evaluation framework. This approach explains the somewhat "scholarly" content of Part I and Part II of the publication. The book avoids setting up a readily applicable blue print for an evaluation framework. Rather than cook-book solutions, it attempts to discuss concepts that can and have to be adapted to the specific situation of a given country or development agency. What is required is a critical analysis by the development manager to identify his information needs and his capacity to use efficiently the information generated. For this reason, many of the terms used in the book need specification at the country or development agency level. For example, the terms project-, programme- and policy management can cover quite different entities in the various countries concerned. It is the task of the development manager to specify those concepts, so that they reflect the reality of the situation with which they are concerned.

The outline of the publication reflects the purpose of the book:

Part I discusses existing project appraisal methodologies. The first Chapter outlines the evolution of the concepts of development and the various terms used in project analysis. Chapter 2 defines the place of project analysis in the planning exercise. Chapter 3 discusses the various appraisal methodologies that are currently proposed in the literature.

Part II outlines a management approach to development activities. The proposed iterative approach considers planning, policy formulation, policy execution and evaluation as an inter-related, circular search process that provides continuously new information on the social development process and thus ameliorates the decision-making process and policy execution alike. Project appraisal/evaluation becomes a management tool, not only for the execution of a particular project but also for the monitoring of social policy and decision-making in general. Social indicators are suggested for collecting and structuring the data required and the different levels of analysis are outlined.

Part III provides a more eclectic and practical approach to project appraisal/evaluation. It is conceded that the management approach outlined in Part II is an ideal which rarely, if ever, exists in a government. The fact is that project evaluations are usually not integrated into a management system. Part III therefore discusses how a useful evaluation system can be set up in the absence of a management system. The approach takes monitoring/evaluation as an entry point to improving the management of social development. Current reporting practices are discussed and their shortcomings outlined. The various steps that have to be undertaken to set up a monitoring/evaluation system at the agency and programme/project level are outlined.

Each part of the book contains a short annotated bibliography that refers to selected works which discuss in more detail some of the concepts treated in the paper.

Part I

PROJECT APPRAISAL METHODOLOGIES

I

INTRODUCTION AND DEFINITIONS

1. Introduction

During the last few years, there has been a growing call for reorientation in the field of development and for the reassessment of societal priorities and goals. Despite economic growth in LDCs, the problems of unemployment, poverty, political and social disaggregation have not been solved. The emphasis has shifted from economic growth to income distribution, from production to the satisfaction of human needs, from technology to the development of human resources.

At the same time, the approach towards the understanding of development has changed. The dissatisfaction with partial models (whether economic or social) has led to a unified approach in which social, political and economic factors are considered within an inter-related systems framework.

The shift in priorities and the better understanding of the causes and dimensions of the problems of LDCs has had two consequences:

- a new philosophy of development putting priority on the human dimension of development. This approach to development recognizes "... that people are the target as well as the essential variable in development, that effective development by and of people requires new approaches to the organisation and management of people and resources - in other words, social policy that creates ways to facilitate and guide change in the direction of goals and objectives valued by the developing society - and, finally, that the creation of successful social policy will depend upon an understanding of what is involved ... and upon the recognition of the need to acquire the data necessary for planning and making decisions. "[1]
- a search for new management tools to assess the operation and impact of public programmes in the social field.

The shift in priorities and the new emphasis on social aspects of development has also called into doubt the usefulness of traditional economic project appraisal and evaluation. To assess the need for new tools of project appraisal/evaluation, it is necessary to determine

1. "Social Systems Models of Indicators of Social Development - A Preliminary Methodological Framework", by Wilcox, Leslie D. et al., Vol. 1, p. 2 (Preliminary Report to USAID), Iowa State University, Ames, Iowa, December 1972.

the differences between more traditional economic projects and the so-called social projects. While there are many differences between activities whose primary objectives are socio-political and projects which primarily address economic goals, there are three basic differences that are important for project appraisal/evaluation:

i) Agreement on expected results

While there is general agreement on economic goals, there exists a lack of agreement on what results social projects are expected to achieve, e.g. everybody would agree that the economic goal of a coffee plantation is to increase coffee production at the least cost possible. There is, however, considerable disagreement about what results an education project should have.

ii) Agreement on means to measure the result

While there is general agreement on how to measure economic results, there exist no generally agreed upon means of knowing whether the expected social results have actually occurred or not, e.g. there is no disagreement that the economic result of a coffee plantation can be measured by the net benefit of the activities; in contrast there exists a whole library of how to measure educational outcomes.

iii) Knowledge about the relationships between inputs and outputs

The production function of coffee production is relatively well known: we know which combination of inputs at what cost will produce a given level of benefits. No such generally applicable production functions exist in the social fields.

Therefore the paper attempts to show:
- how these three basic differences affect the applicability of economic project appraisal methodology to more social concerns;
- how these additional problems of project appraisal/evaluation could be handled.

However, before that, it is necessary to define some of the concepts used in the paper.

2. Definitions

Terms in project appraisal/evaluation are not yet well standardised. Certain terms are associated with specific methodologies. For example, social cost-benefit analysis is mostly associated with the methodology of calculating shadow prices to value inputs and outputs of a project, despite the fact that the goal of any project appraisal methodology is to analyse the social costs and benefits of a project. Other terms refer to concepts that are not specified. The terms of goal, objective, purpose are often not differentiated; project appraisal/evaluation are used interchangeably. This uncertainty about what the various terms mean creates a certain confusion. It is therefore necessary to define the most common concepts used in this paper.

i) Project

Project in this paper is defined as any actual or planned activity that is the object of an appraisal/evaluation exercise. Since in a project appraisal/evaluation exercise we are interested in the effects of the "project" on society, we define project as the smallest unit (activity, decision), the impact of which on the society can be isolated. If the impact of a set of activities on the society "is indecomposable, that is, their total impact is different from the sum of their impact as separate projects"[1], then the set of activities has to be considered as the object or "project" of the appraisal/evaluation exercise.

Thus the object of a project appraisal/evaluation can be an activity (project), a set of inter-related activities (programme) or a decision (policy).

The boundaries of an appraisal/evaluation exercise depend on the use of the appraisal/evaluation results and on the decision level considered. Within a hierarchical decision-making structure, the decisions of a higher decision level determine the boundaries of a lower decision level and thus limit the scope of the appraisal/evaluation.[2] The appraisal/evaluation has to concentrate on the factors that the user of the results can influence, e. g. an appraisal/evaluation of a Maternity and Child Health Clinic for the Ministry of Health would question the purpose of the clinic, the amount of money spent on those clinics compared to other health activities, etc. The same evaluation for the Director of a regional health centre might not question the allocation of resources to Maternity and Child Health Clinics, as he cannot influence this decision. The evaluation would "accept" the amount of resources and staff attributed to the clinic and try to determine how to given investment can best be utilised (out-patients versus in-patients;

---

1. A. Papandreou, Uri Zohar: National Planning and Socio-Economic Priorities. The Impact Approach to Project Selection, Vol. II, p. 39, Praeger, 1974.

In "Project Selection for National Plans", Vol. I, the same authors define the unit of appraisal in abstract terms (pp. 23-26):

M = programme

$P_1, P_2 \ldots P_N$ = projects part of a programme

$d(M)$ = impact of programme

$d(P_n)$ = impact of programme

$$d_{(M)} \neq d_{(P_1)} + d_{(P_2)} \ldots + d_{(P_N)}.$$

2. For more details on the influence of the level of decision-making on the boundaries of the appraisal, see Stefan A. Musto, "Evaluierung sozialer Entwicklungsprojekte", DIE, Bruno Hessling Verlag, 1972, pp. 29-48.

pre-natal versus post-natal activities, etc.). The Director of the Clinic might not have the choice of allocating the time and money spent within the different activities. An appraisal/evaluation for him would there-fore consider the alternative activities (pre-natal, post-natal, infant care) as given, and address the question of how each activity can best be executed. He expects the evaluation to address the relationship between inputs and outputs.

ii) Project appraisal

Project appraisal is the analysis of costs and benefits of a propos-ed project with the goal of assuring a rational allocation of limited funds among alternative investment opportunities in view of achieving certain specified goals.

Project appraisal is necessary as the number of projects to satisfy the identified needs exceeds the resources available. It is therefore necessary to make a choice among alternative projects. A choice implies necessarily a comparison of different alternatives.

Project appraisal can be divided into two steps:

- The identification of the effects of the project

Before we can determine the value of an action, we have to determine the probable effects of that action. While the effects of certain actions are relatively easy to predict (it is relatively simple to predict the effects of a given hydropower plant on the total elec-tricity production of a country), the effects of other actions are much less amenable to predictions (e. g. the effects of a new curriculum on the cognitive ability of the school children).

- The valuation of these effects

Whether the identified effects of a project are desirable (i. e. , are considered as benefits) or not (i. e. , have to be considered as a cost) depends on the goals pursued by the society. It is possible that the same effect constitutes a benefit and a cost at the same time. An increase in agricultural production is a benefit if we consider growth as the major goal of society. This same increase of production might, however, be a cost if a more equitable income distribution is a major goal of the society. This double counting of an effect is not a contradiction: it is the consequence of valuing the same object by different objectives that are not necessarily compatible in a given situation.

The relative importance given to these two steps of project appraisal depends on our knowledge about the production process. For certain economic effects, valuation will be the primary task of project appraisal, while the identification of the effects of non-directly productive projects will be the primary purpose of the social analysis.

14

iii) Project appraisal/evaluation

Project appraisal and project evaluation are two aspects of the same analytical exercise:

- project appraisal is the ex-ante analysis of a proposed project. It identifies and values the expected costs and benefits of a project. The expected results of a project are based on an analysis of the functioning of the project and of its inter-relationships with the socio-economic environment. The determination of the effects of a project is always based on some more-or-less verified hypotheses;
- project evaluation is the ex-post analysis of an executed project. It determines the real benefits provided by the project and establishes the effective costs incurred by the project. By comparing the expected project results (ex-ante) with the real results (ex-post), project evaluation tests the hypotheses established during the appraisal exercise.

The inter-relationship between the two analysis is evident:

- rigorous project evaluation is very difficult if it is not known what sort of results were initially expected. Project appraisal thus provides project evaluation with the necessary information on:
  - the specific results the project is expected to have;
  - the information necessary to determine the success/failure of the project;
  - the yardsticks to be used to determine the success or failure of the project;
  - the hypotheses that have to be verified;

- meaningful project appraisal, on the other hand, depends on a minimum of knowledge about the production process and the environment in which the project is supposed to function. Project evaluation contributes to a better project appraisal by:
  - providing information on results that can or cannot be expected from specific interventions;
  - providing information on the functioning of the society;
  - specifying the hypotheses on which the calculations of benefits and costs are based.

In view of this interdependence, it is necessary to execute and discuss the two analyses within the same framework. For this reason we use the term "project appraisal/evaluation" if the concepts discussed are the same for the two exercises.

iv) Project appraisal methodology

Methods of project appraisal are the analytical frameworks used to assure the optimum allocation of scarce resources to achieve a defined goal or set of goals.

15

The only rational method of allocating limited resources among a number of alternative activities is to choose the projects that achieve the identified goal or set of goals at the minimal cost possible, or that obtain the highest degree of goal achievement with the given resources available.

Any project appraisal methodology is therefore a cost-benefit analysis: a project is accepted if its net benefits exceed those of the next best alternative course of action. If such an investment criterion is applied to all possible solutions and if all alternatives are taken into account, the projects chosen will generate the largest possible benefits within the constraints given in a specific society.

As Cases points out: "The idea of optimisation (i.e. the search for the 'best' result arising from the comparison of alternatives by reference to a certain criterion of desirability) cannot be eliminated from a society where scarcity remains the rule: even if missing costs and benefits are reintroduced by means of accounting which can, if one wishes, be described as 'social', a mechanism for the allocation of resources which adjusts the supply and use of resources is still necessary. The insufficiencies of economic calculation therefore cannot result in its elimination, but they are in the process of contributing to its revision."[1]

Thus there is a general agreement on what a project appraisal methodology is supposed to achieve. However, the methodologies differ on how to calculate the benefits and costs and how to determine the "optimality" of a proposed action.

- Costs and benefits: Costs and benefits cannot be determined in abstracto. The costs and benefits of a project can only be fixed within the concrete setting in which the project is executed. The costs and benefits of the same project may vary therefore according to:
  - the relative factor endowment in a country. The costs and benefits depend not only on physical and financial factors, but also on political, social and cultural constraints;
  - the objectives set by the country. Since objective setting is a political act and since costs and benefits can only be determined according to the objectives set, there is a certain voluntaristic element in defining the costs and benefits of a project. This voluntaristic element in the determination of costs and benefits is seldom explicitly recognised.

- "Optimality": "Optimality" as used in this paper is not considered as an abstract, objective criterion. An action is considered "optimal" if there is no alternative, feasible action that can achieve the same goal or set of goals at less or the same cost. However,

1. Bernard Cases: "The development of social indicators: A survey" in "Social Indicators and Social Policy", p. 18, Andrew Shonfield and Stella Shaw (eds.), Heineman Educational Books, London, 1972.

which alternative actions are considered feasible depends on the subjective appreciation of what is economically, socially and politically feasible. Thus a land reform might be the optimal means to achieve a desired income distribution. However, land reform might not be considered politically feasible, hence the next best alternative becomes "optimal" for the decision-makers.

v) Social or non-directly productive projects

The distinction between economic and social projects cannot be drawn according to the effects of a project. Economic projects do have a social impact and social projects are not irrelevant to economic growth. On the basis of a study on the correlation among development indicators, UNRISD concludes: "the available data do not lend support to the view that there is a general economic factor of development and a separate social factor."[1] The distinction between economic and social projects is therefore a matter of emphasis rather than of substance: the primary goals of social projects are socio-political, while economic projects' primary goals are economic growth. Therefore, the concepts of directly productive and non-directly productive projects are more accurate than economic and social projects.

3. A methodology for the appraisal of non-directly productive projects

As economic and social factors are inter-dependent, it is dangerous to compartmentalise development even for the purpose of analysis. Too often has so-called economic analysis wrongly ignored the social implications of projects. At the same time, social services, characterised by heavy costs of recurrent expenditure and long gestation periods, cannot be analysed without reference to the productive sector that will have to provide the necessary resources to pay and maintain those services.[2]

To avoid misallocation of resources, it is therefore necessary to adopt an integrated approach to project appraisal/evaluation and to use the same criteria and methodological framework for non-directly productive and directly productive projects alike.

However, since the methodological problems in measuring and evaluating the social effects of a project differ from the measurement problems of its economic effects, it makes sense to distinguish:

---

1. UNRISD, Research Notes No. 1: "Review of recent and current studies conducted at the Institute", Geneva, 1968, p. 11.

2. For an analysis and examples of social projects that have neglected certain economic aspects, see The Design of Rural Development: Lessons from Africa, Uma Lélé, IBRD, A World Bank Research Publication, The Johns Hopkins University Press, Baltimore and London, 1975.

- the economic effects of a project, i. e. , the effects that are
directly related to the goal of income creation and the costs
and benefits of which can be expressed in monetary terms;
- the social effects of a project, i. e. , the effects that are related
to other goals than income creation and that include values,
attitudes, goods and services that cannot necessarily be expressed in commensurable terms.

It is the intention of this paper to concentrate on the methodological
problems of social effects within a general framework of project
analysis.

i) Project appraisal and objectives

It is not the task of project appraisal per se to define objectives.
Objectives should be defined at the policy and programme level. However, very often the objectives defined at the policy and programme
level are not explicit enough to link the project objectives to those higher
level goals. Because of the close relation of costs and benefits to the
objectives, project appraisal has to analyse the different objectives
pursued by the various proposed projects. To be able to judge the
contribution of the output of a micro project (e. g. , the training of
drilling teams) to a general development goal (e. g. , improving health
conditions in rural areas), it is necessary to establish intermediate
goals (e. g. trained drillers ⟶ efficient environmental health department ⟶ increased water supply ⟶ use of clean water ⟶
better health), i. e. it is necessary to establish a hierarchy of goals.

ii) Goals hierarchy

For the purpose of this paper, we use the following terminology
and hierarchy among objectives:

- goals: the term goal is used to indicate overall development
directions. Goals indicate desired ends that are an expression of the
society's value system. They include such goals as "increase in
consumption", "equitable income distribution", "quality of life",
"independence", "self-reliance", etc. They can be considered as the
social, structural and economic variables constituting the development
function that decision-makers want to maximise.[1]

- objectives: they are the expression of the goals at a lower level
of abstraction. The achievement of an objective contributes to the
attainment of one or more of the goal variables. The objectives are
normally expressed at the sector level, e. g. , to increase the life

---

1. Social cost benefit analysis assumes that the main objectives can be expressed in two
ultimate societal goals: consumption and income distribution. All other objectives
(health, education, self-reliance, etc.) are only partial so that each objective can be
evaluated according to its contribution to the achievement of those two basic goals.

expectancy at birth to 60 years by 1980 for the health sector; to provide a functional primary education to 90% of the school-aged children by 1980, for education, etc.

- purpose: purposes are operational objectives that have to be achieved to fulfil the sectoral objectives, e. g. , to achieve the health objective it is necessary to decrease the incidence of environmental health hazards by 20%, to decrease infant mortality by 50% and to eradicate malaria.

- targets: they are specific quantified results that have to be met to achieve the purposes, e. g. , to decrease the environmental health hazards by 20% it might be necessary to achieve the following targets: to increase the population served by safe drinking water from 50% to 75%; to provide safe excreta disposal to 500,000 additional people; to provide information on hygiene to 50% of the school children, etc.

- outputs: are physical products that have to be produced to fulfil the targets, e.g. , to provide 75% of the population with safe drinking water it might be necessary to install 1,500 handpumps, 2,000 stand-points and 20 distribution systems for towns with a population of 15,000.

- inputs: inputs are the various factors of production that have to be provided to produce the output: e. g. to install the 1,500 handpumps, it might be necessary to import two drilling rigs, to train 5 drilling teams, to undertake a hydrogeological survey, etc.

II

PLANNING, PROJECT SELECTION, APPRAISAL AND EVALUATION

1. Introduction

While there exists considerable disagreement of how to appraise, manage and evaluate development activities, the need for a systematic management system is unquestioned.

The criticisms against project analysis can be summed up under the following headings[1]:

- Disagreement with the basic philosophy of the methodologies proposed

The administrations in less developed countries often feel that the specific management methods proposed do not take into account sufficiently their own objectives. They feel that many of the underlying assumptions of specific methodologies have been derived from a traditional western approach and are not justified in the LDC environment.

- Disagreement about the usefulness of the methodologies proposed

LDC administrations are often not convinced that the proposed analytical methods lead to better decision-making and management. They often consider appraisal methods as window dressing to make decisions already made acceptable to some foreign donor, and proposed monitoring systems as a means of hidden controls imposed by foreign interest groups. Since management systems are mostly proposed and often imposed by foreign donors, they are considered as just one other means of control used by foreign powers.

- Disagreement about the applicability of the methodologies proposed

It is contended that most methodologies proposed are not taking into account the institutional and organisational aspects of the countries

_____

1. This is a summary of the interventions made by LDC representatives at the "Meeting of experts on project appraisal" organised by the OECD in Copenhagen on the 8-10 October, 1975. See "Meeting of Experts on Project Appraisal: Summary", Working Document DD 475, Paris, OECD, February 1976.

concerned and often misjudge the decision-making structure. The methods are analytically complex and are too demanding in terms of data and planning capacity. They do not take into account the realities of staffing, time pressure and data availability in less developed countries.

- Disagreement about the questions addressed by the proposed methodologies

According to LDC administrators, the proposed methodologies put too much emphasis on predicting the effects of projects and not enough on the problems of execution and implementation. Moreover, the proposed methodologies concentrate on choices among alternative actions, while LDCs' major concern is to identify those actions. The methodologies attempt to identify optimal solutions to given problems, while LDC administrations are concerned to identify problems and to find satisfying solutions to them.

All these criticisms concern the questions addressed by the proposed analytical systems and the lack of adaptation of the methodologies proposed to the real world situation. They do not question the need for a management system for development projects. They do, however, suggest that a management system should comprise the whole project cycle (from the identification of a problem to the verification of the result of the proposed solution to that problem) and not analyse projects in isolation.

2. Project appraisal/evaluation as part of a development management system

Project appraisal/evaluation cannot be considered in isolation. They are part of a larger management system of development efforts. The costs and benefits of an appraisal/evaluation methodology depend on the inputs they receive from other parts of the management system and from the use that the management system makes of their output.

i) The planning exercise

Governments are engaged in planning, i.e., they deliberately manipulate a number of means at their disposal to attain certain aims.[1] The Government's planning exercise implies:

- a set of implicit or explicit goals;

---

1. See J. Tinbergen: Economic Policy: Principles and Design, 1964, p. 6. North Holland Publishing Co. Amsterdam, 1956.

- some understanding of the development of the social trajectory[1] over time;
- the belief that the development of the social trajectory does not automatically lead to the achievement of the stated societal goals;
- the belief that there exist alternative feasible social trajectories that correspond more closely to the societal goals and that can be brought about by policy interventions.

All this information is taken into account, explicitly or implicitly, in any planning exercise. As McKean points out: "Systematic thought about any problem of choice necessarily involves models, naive or otherwise."[2]

The planning effort can thus be considered as a "process whereby all relevant information is utilised to formulate a method of implementation that will achieve the desired objectives".[3]

There are different steps involved in a planning exercise and each step has its particular information requirements, its agents and its outputs:

a) Policy planning: The purpose of the policy planning exercise is to determine general guidelines that should lead to the fulfilment of overall development goals. The policy planning exercise needs information on the overall socio-economic development, on production capacities of the different sectors, their inter-relationships and on the

---

1. Social trajectory is the description of the state of society over time, defined in terms of the values assumed by the variables that are considered necessary and sufficient to describe the development of the society.

Papandreou and Zohar express the social trajectory with a matrix of social indicators.

$$W_{(mt)} = \begin{bmatrix} W_{11} & W_{12} & W_{1t} & W_{1T} \\ W_{21} & W_{22} & W_{mt} & W_{2T} \\ W_{m1} & W_{m2} & W_{mt} & W_{mT} \\ W_{M1} & W_{M2} & W_{Mt} & W_{MT} \end{bmatrix}$$

W_{mt} = the value of the mth (socially relevant indicator) at time t.

M = number of indicators necessary to describe the social trajectory.

T = time periods considered.

See Papandreou/Zohar, op. cit., Vol. I, p. 13, and Vol. II, p. 33 ff.

2. Roland N. McKean: Efficiency in Government through Systems Analysis, Rand Corporation Research No.3, 1958, p. 5. John Wiley and Sons, New York.

3. Denis Warner: "Evaluation of Development Impact of Rural Water Supply Projects in East African Villages", December 1973, Report EEP, Standford University (Ph. D. Dissertation).

22

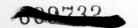

resources (financial, human and institutional) that can be mobilised. The policy planning consists of the specification of sectoral objectives: it provides the link between sectoral objectives and overall development goals of the society. It determines the relative weight of the various sectoral objectives and the overall resource allocation between them. It is essentially a political exercise and should be executed by the highest political levels.

b) Sectoral planning: Analyses the alternative sectoral strategies that would lead to the achievement of the objectives specified by the policy planning exercise and attempts to select the best one. Sectoral planning needs more specific information about the problems, functioning, resources and constraints of the sector concerned. Sectoral planning needs to be done by the top management of the technical services of the specific administration. It will provide the link between the programme purposes and the sectoral objectives and define the resources available to each programme.

c) Programme planning: Will attempt to determine the services needed (targets) to achieve the chosen purposes of the various programmes identified in the sectoral plan. Programme planning needs very specific information at a rather disaggregated level. It will probably be executed within each Directorate of the technical agency (Ministry) concerned. The product of a programme planning exercise is a list of interrelated activities and services that have to be provided.

d) Project appraisal: Identifies the activities and products necessary to provide the services identified in the programme. The appraisal stage needs guidelines from the higher level planning efforts and a close knowledge of project activities, resources, bottlenecks and potentials. The output will be a detailed analysis of projects (output, process input) that are submitted for execution.

ii) The implementation phase

Once policies, programmes and projects are approved, they have to be implemented. The implementation phase implies the following tasks:[1]

a) Monitoring of the execution: The purpose of a monitoring system is to provide the necessary information for effective project or programme management. It consists of accounting, auditing and reporting. It tries to compare planned outputs, targets, purpose with the real levels achieved by the project. Monitoring is supposed to determine what has happened, not why it has happened. What

_____

1. The steps to be undertaken in the implementation phase are discussed in detail in part III "Setting up a monitoring/evaluation system for social programmes".

to include into a monitoring system depends on the management level concerned: a project manager is requested to monitor inputs and outputs; a programme manager targets and purpose; a sector manager purpose and objective, and a planning agency objectives and goals.

b) Process evaluation: Is the task of adapting a project, programme or sector plan during implementation, when the monitoring information shows that such changes are indicated. Process evaluation distinguishes itself from monitoring by two factors:

- process evaluation is a discontinuous activity; it is only undertaken when the monitoring information shows that activities and results are not matched by the actual results. Process evaluation attempts to define why things happen the way they do. Monitoring is a continuous activity and provides information on what happens. The boundaries of process evaluation again depend on the management level concerned.

c) Ex-post evaluation: The purpose of ex-post evaluation is to provide the necessary feedback of the lessons learned to the planning stage. It is supposed to provide better information for the analysis and planning. Ex-post evaluation validates or invalidates the assumptions on which the planning exercise was based or, if programmes have not been defined in a very rigorous way, ex-post evaluation permits to delimit the problems in a more precise way (formative evaluation).

The different phases in the management system are interdependent and each phase is dependent on the other steps to provide the inputs to the analysis. (Figure I).

iii) The role of project appraisal in the management system

As has been shown, project appraisal is only one link in the whole planning exercise. To implement their planning goals, Governments have to take a multitude of micro decisions at various organisational levels. To assure consistency between the national development plan and the micro decisions, it is necessary to systematically relate each micro decision to the general development goals. This is the role of project appraisal methodology.

3. The information needs of a project appraisal exercise

The information needs for project appraisal are large. It is necessary:
- to know how the society is developing without public intervention;
- to determine the desirable outcome of the development process, i.e., development goals have to be defined;
- to compare the desirable outcome of the development process with the probable result of the society's natural development;

24

Figure I. MANAGEMENT SYSTEM FOR DEVELOPMENT ACTIVITIES

	INPUTS	OUTPUTS	GOAL LEVEL	ADMINISTRATION LEVEL	EXAMPLE
Policy Planning	- Analysis theory values information on sectors	- L. T. Development Plan - Link: goals-objectives - Relative importance of sectors and allocation of resources	Goals	Ministry of Planning (advice from technical Ministries)	Removal of poverty → Education, etc., Production; Health
Sectoral Planning	- Draft Plan - Resource allocations to sector - Information on alternative strategies	- A sectoral strategy - Link: objectives-purpose - Relative importance of programmes and allocation of resources	Objective	Technical Ministries (Ministry of Education)	Provide equal access to education for rural population; Increase primary enrollment ratio from 60 to 70% of school aged children
Programme Planning	- Sectoral strategy - Resource allocations to various programmes - Information on projects	- A programme - Link: purpose-targets - Relative importance of projects and allocation of resources	Purpose	Directorate of Technical Ministries (Director of Primary Education)	Increase primary enrollment ratio from 50 to 70%; Curricula reform
Project Appraisal	- Programme - Resource allocations between various projects - Information on relations between outputs and targets	- Service to be provided - Link: target-output - Relative importance of output for target - Link: output-input	Target / Output	Directorate of Technical Ministries and Consultants	Double output of vocational training institutes; Construction of 500 new classrooms; Training of 300 new primary school teachers/year
Project Execution	- Project description - Link input-output - Definition of project components	- A project management framework - A monitoring/evaluation framework	Inputs	Project Director and staff	Production of teaching material for all classes in science
Project Evaluation	- Management information - Monitoring information	- Assessment of project's net benefits - Assessment of project's logic - Tests of the hypotheses		Different levels according to type of evaluation	

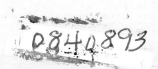

- to define alternative development trajectories that correspond more closely to the desired development outcome than the country's given development trajectory;
- to determine which alternative development trajectories are feasible given the economic, political and social constraints of the country;
- to determine the costs and benefits of alternative means available;
- to determine the optimal mix of means to achieve the desired development trajectory.

In a planning system such as the one described above, project appraisal will obtain most of the information required from the other planning steps.

As Figure II indicates, project appraisal depends on the other analysis for the identification of goals and their operationalisation. What is even more important, the project appraisal exercise requires that the other analyses identify alternative strategies, sector plans and programmes.

Thus project appraisal is not the central focus at which health, education, and productive projects are compared. Before project appraisal starts, numerous decisions have already been taken, alternatives considered and rejected. [1] Project appraisal thus consists of a scrutiny of a limited number of projects that have been chosen from a much larger set of alternative actions. It is the detailed analysis of a few micro decisions to assure their consistency with national development goals.

4.   Different types of project appraisal

It is clear that the management system described above corresponds to an ideal situation, which is rarely (or never) found in the real world. It is possible that in a given situation the policy planning exercise has been omitted. It is then up to the sector planners to interpret the fractionary information available on values and directions cherished by the policy makers and to translate them into development goals to which the sectoral objectives can be linked. Sector plans may, however, be very vague, consisting of a description of major inputs in the sector without defining objectives or alternative programmes. In another situation there may exist programmes which consist of a description of a proposed programme without a critical analysis of alternative activities that might achieve the same objectives at a lower resource cost. In such cases, project appraisal cannot rely on the information from the other planning phases as described in Figure II. Project appraisal will

---

1.   Such a procedure assures that project alternatives are considered at a very early stage. Many feasible alternatives are eliminated at the level of project idea and project identification.

Figure II. PROJECT APPRAISAL IN A MANAGEMENT SYSTEM

Inputs from higher level analysis

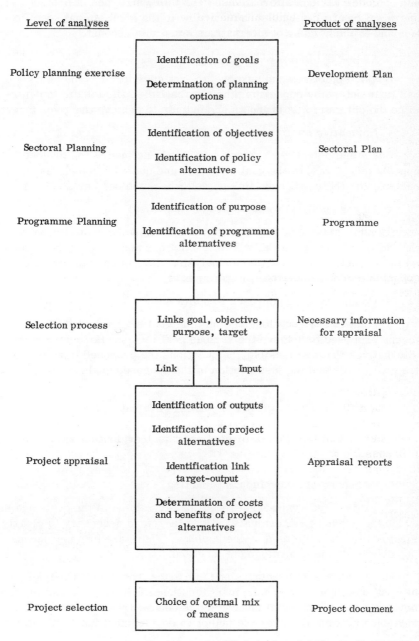

Level of analyses		Product of analyses
Policy planning exercise	Identification of goals Determination of planning options	Development Plan
Sectoral Planning	Identification of objectives Identification of policy alternatives	Sectoral Plan
Programme Planning	Identification of purpose Identification of programme alternatives	Programme
Selection process	Links goal, objective, purpose, target	Necessary information for appraisal
	Link Input	
Project appraisal	Identification of outputs Identification of project alternatives Identification link target-output Determination of costs and benefits of project alternatives	Appraisal reports
Project selection	Choice of optimal mix of means	Project document

N.B. Such a step-wise analysis assures that project appraisal is limited to the analysis of comparable alternatives (i.e., projects within a given programme) and is not required to compare projects which are not comparable at the appraisal stage (e.g., an airport project compared to a project of rural health).

thus have to be comprehensive and attempt to fill the gaps in earlier analyses. It will have to question the programmes and the strategies and consider various alternatives. The following types of project appraisal can be distinguished according to the level of goal specification and to the number of alternatives taken into account.[1]

- Functional project appraisal

Goals, objectives and purpose are not questioned. The appraisor has little autonomy concerning the alternatives. His task is to determine the optimum mix of inputs and outputs to achieve the given targets.

- Normative approach to appraisal

Goals and objectives are not sufficiently defined. The project appraisor will review the goal structure and question objectives and purposes or their proposed link if, and when, the need arises.

- Incremental approach to project appraisal

The appraisor can only consider a limited number of alternatives that do not vary considerably from the actions and programmes proposed in the sector and programme analysis. He has no authority over the main components of the programme.

- Comprehensive approach to appraisal

The appraisor questions not only the goal hierarchy but also the means proposed to achieve the various goal levels. He considers all alternatives that are feasible, he questions the proposed links between the goal levels and the justification of the proposed goals.

5. The difficulties of a project appraisal/evaluation exercise

The main difficulties of project appraisal/evaluation are due to the following facts:

i) Absence of a development function

Appraisal and evaluation are intimately related to the goals against which the projects are evaluated. It is therefore necessary to clearly identify the goals pursued by the society. There are two approaches possible to define a development function:

a) Elaboration of theories and inference from theoretical definitions of what should enter a development function: This approach attempts to develop a theory of social change and to deduce from that theory the variables that should enter the objective development function. However,

---

1. Adapted from "Health Programme Planning and Project Selection" by Guido J. Deboeck and M. A. Piot, 1975, WHO, GVA International Papers, PSA/EC/75.6(a).

development is inevitably a normative concept and therefore value-loaded. The existence of different values within a society and the question of whose values are supposed to be expressed, explain our inability to formulate collective or social goals that reflect a society's values.[1] While abstract general goals that seem reasonable, desirable and universally acceptable can be found, they are invariably too general to provide the necessary criteria for project appraisal. Even if an agreement on general development goals could be found - this should be possible where the basic human needs are not fulfilled - once you pass from general to specific goals the operational alternatives expand and the conflict of interests flare up again. Therefore, the development of a general development theory is hampered by:
- the value-loaded character of the concept of development;
- the existence of competing value systems within each society;
- the dependence of development objectives on the needs and problems of each society and on the realistic assessment of the resources available to the society;
- the subjectivity of the determination of a set of feasible social development paths.

E. g. , the definition of an equitable income distribution and its relative importance as a development goal depends on:
- the specific philosophy and value system of the person concerned: socialism, capitalism, traditionalism all have quite different opinions of what level of income differentials can be tolerated;
- who is asked to define "equitable income distribution: it is quite probable that the different social strata have rather different concepts about what an equitable income distribution means;
- the existing income distribution in the country and on the possibilities the country has of improving the situation. A country having a high growth rate and a very skewed income distribution is probably ready to pay a higher price for income redistribution than a country with a stagnant economy and relatively moderate inequalities;
- what actions are considered feasible to change the income distribution. If a land reform is considered feasible, it is obviously possible to pursue much higher distributional goals than if such action is considered as unfeasible. A landless labourer would probably assess the feasibility of land reform rather differently than a parliamentarian.

b) The inductive method tries to develop a general development theory from the observation and analysis of actual development processes. However, it is impossible to derive a development theory from statistical analysis of observed changes in the socio-economic field as those

---

1. For a discussion of class conflict and preference functions, see Francis Stewart: "A note on social cost-benefit analysis and class conflicts in LDCs' in World Development, Vol. 3, No.1, January 1975, pp. 31-39.

methods provide only correlations or correspondance points among chosen variables. To infer from statistical data a causality or an optimal development pattern, it is necessary to have a theoretical framework derived from the definition of development, e. g. we know that the rain-agricultural production relationship is a causal one, not simply because they correlate, but because we have a theory of how plants grow and which inputs are needed to make them grow.

This impasse in the construction of the development function is of great importance for project appraisal. If an objective development function could be constructed, project appraisal could be objective, as the maximisation of this objective function would give us an unambiguous objective criterion for investment decisions that would be unique for all projects whether directly productive or not.

ii) The absence of a model for a goal matrix

The link between different goal levels is always a hypothetical one, e. g. there is no agreement on how rural water supply influences health standards or what education contributes to increases in productivity of the labour force. In the absence of explicit hypotheses, it is thus very difficult to judge the validity of an appraisal exercise and impossible to reconstruct the reasoning later at the evaluation stage.

6. Desirable characteristics of a project appraisal methodology

From the discussion so far, we can define the desirable characteristics of a project appraisal methodology:

i) Development cannot be compartmentalised into economic, political and social development. A project appraisal methodology has therefore to be an integrated framework.

ii) The outcome of project appraisal heavily depends on the goals pursued and the alternatives considered. A project appraisal methodology has therefore to provide an organic link between country programming, sectoral analysis, project identification and project appraisal per se.

iii) The definition of development goals is not objective. A project appraisal methodology has to specifically state the assumptions made and make explicit the values implied in the chosen development function.

iv) Project appraisal presupposes an understanding of the social framework. Since there are hardly any models available to define the effects of a project on the social development, the project appraisor relies on implicit theories and hypotheses to determine the effects of a project. To make the project appraisal retraceable and to allow the checking of the theories and assumptions, it is necessary that a project appraisal methodology:

- makes assumptions and theories explicit;
- defines the expected project's effects in a verifiable way;
- defines the means of verification of theory and assumptions.

v) Most project appraisal methodologies are tailored to the requirements of specific objectives and to the characteristics of policy instruments. However, objectives and policy instruments change through time: our knowledge about socio-economic development increases and new means of socio-economic intervention become available. It is therefore necessary that an analytical framework is general enough, so that new knowledge about the socio-economic change can be incorporated with the project appraisal framework.

Moreover the different uses made of project appraisal methodology allows the determination of desirable further characteristics.

vi) Project appraisal/evaluation methodology as a management tool for decision-makers. To be useful as a management tool, the methodology has to be adapted to the decision-making process in a given organisation. The desirability and utility of an appraisal methodology depend on the goodness of the fit between skills (planning methodologies), tools (statistics or indicators available) and desired output (objectives) in a given country. It is clear that the levels of skills, the knowledge and information of the socio-economic situation vary from country to country. A general project appraisal methodology has therefore to be a general framework of information gathering that can be adapted to the local situation, rather than a specific technique requiring predetermined information and skills that might not be available.

vii) Project appraisal methodology as a management tool for the implementation of projects. Because of our limited knowledge of the socio-economic development process, the determination of a project's effects are accompanied by important uncertainties. A project appraisal methodology should provide the necessary information to help the management of the project execution by:
- determining the sensitivities of the project outcome to the proposed assumptions;
- identifying key variables that have to be closely monitored;
- determining the information needs to closely monitor the project execution;
- providing the necessary flexibility in the project design to adapt the projects to unforeseen developments or to new insight into the development process. [1]

---

1. Since the appraisal of costs and benefits depends on the assumptions made about the execution of the project, project design has to be part of the appraisal exercise.

viii) Project appraisal/evaluation as a tool for policy information. To fulfil that function, the methodology should:
- provide information on the relationship between macro planning and micro decisions;
- provide analytical information on the development process at the micro level;
- provide information on the significance and effectiveness of policies by providing the necessary information for ex post evaluation of the effects of the project;
- install an information system that provides from project experience the necessary feedback to increase the Government's ability to formulate goals to determine alternative feasible social trajectories and to adopt relevant development policies.

One might think that the demands put upon project appraisal are too high. However, if one admits - and most people do - that the factual and theoretical knowledge about development is far too limited to provide an acceptable basis for project appraisal, the expansion of our knowledge about development becomes first priority. There are two ways of increasing our knowledge about development in general or about the functioning of a particular society:
- basic research and data gathering: while basic research is certainly necessary, it is costly and time consuming. The problems of LDCs are so pressing that it is not possible to wait until research provides the necessary information;
- learning by doing: projects and policies are considered as experiments and used to increase our knowledge about the functioning of the society. Such an approach puts high demands on project appraisal and evaluation. If projects were seen within such a framework by all donor countries, the chances of foreign aid having the catalytic effect it always pretends to have would increase substantially as it would improve the allocation of all the resources of LDCs.

III

PROJECT APPRAISAL METHODOLOGIES

The identification of desirable characteristics permits us to
evaluate various appraisal methodologies not only in terms of their
theoretical value but also according to the functions a project appraisal/
evaluation methodology is supposed to fulfil.

1. Social cost-benefit analysis

There are various methodological frameworks to appraise projects
by using social cost-benefit analysis. However, they are all based on
the same concepts and, as Deepak Lal has shown ". . . any substantive
differences among the alternative procedures are in large part dependent upon differing assumptions".[1]

i) The origins of social cost-benefit analysis

Social cost-benefit analysis has its origin in financial analysis.
A private investor confronted with the choice of alternative investments
determines the profitability of the investments. Cost-benefit analysis
assesses the benefits and costs of alternative investment possibilities
and reduces them to a common denominator. The methodology provides
a simple and seducing criterion for investment decisions: a project is
accepted if its net benefits exceed those of the next best alternative
course of action. If such an investment criterion is applied to all
possible decisions, and if all alternatives are taken into account, this
project appraisal methodology will generate the largest possible
benefits within the given constraints. The definition of costs and
benefits is simple for a private investor: monetary expenditure is
considered as costs and income as a benefit. Thus financial analysis
which "identifies the money profit accruing to the project-operating
entity"[2] provides a private entrepreneur with the necessary criterion to
choose among alternative investments.

---

1. Deepak Lal: "Methods of Project Analysis: A Review", World Bank Staff Occasional
Papers, No.16, 1974, Washington.
2. Lyn Squire, Herman G. van der Tak: Economic Analysis of Projects, A World Bank
Research Publication, John Hopkins University Press, 1975, Baltimore.

Social cost-benefit analysis differs from cost-benefit analysis insofar as the effects of the project are not evaluated according to their profitability to the operating entity but according to their impact on the society as a whole.

Thus social cost-benefit analysis is similar in form to financial analysis: they both assess the profit of an investment. However, they differ in what they consider as a cost and what they consider as a benefit, i. e. , the concept of financial profit is not the same as the social profit. If private benefits would coincide with social profits, there would be no need for two distinct analyses. However, for that to be the case, a host of assumptions concerning full employment, competition, marginality, consumer sovereignity, external effects and income distribution have to be fulfilled.[1] Since those assumptions are normally not justified in less developed countries, social cost-benefit analysis adjusts the financial analysis by:[2]

- including (excluding) some costs and benefits which have been excluded (included) in the financial analysis (e. g. transfer payments, contingencies, sunk costs, externalities, multiplier effects, etc.);
- revaluing certain inputs/outputs according to shadow prices reflecting their real cost-benefit rather than their market value, e. g. rather than using the market price of labour, social cost-benefit would calculate the opportunity cost, i. e. the marginal output of labour forgone elsewhere because of its use in the project.

Thus traditional social cost-benefits analysis has been evaluating projects according to a single objective, i. e. the increase of income to the society without giving sufficient attention to other social objectives a society may pursue. Most criticism against social cost-benefit analysis is addressed to this type of analysis.

ii)   The inclusion of distributional objectives into social cost-benefit analysis

More recent publications[3] include income distribution and other social objectives more explicitly in the calculation of the benefits of the project. Thus the social income of a project, i. e. the net increase in output of the economy which the project brings about, is no longer considered as the measure of the project's value to the society. To

---

1.   J. M. D. Little and J. A. Mirrlees: Project Appraisal and Planning for Developing Countries, Heinemann Educational Books, London 1974, pp. 19-24 discuss the different assumptions.

2.   Lyn Squire, op. cit., pp. 19-25 discusses the factors which have to be excluded/ included in social cost-benefit analysis compared to financial analysis.

3.   The two most recent publications on this subject are the two mentioned in footnote 2 (page 33) and footnote 1 above.

determine the project's value to the society "... we must consider the use to which the social income is put. " (Thus) "the social income will be corrected to allow for the disadvantages of being committed to consumption by particular income groups. "[1] In the same way, Squire and van der Tak determine the value of inputs and outputs of a project not only in terms of technical and behavioural parameters but also according to value judgements made by the Government: "Shadow prices are here defined as the value of the contribution to the country's basic socio-economic objectives made by any marginal change in the availability of commodities or factors of production. "... "Any changes in objectives or constraints will therefore necessitate a change in the estimated shadow prices. "[2] Thus the process of shadow pricing presupposes a clear understanding of the country's objectives and their interrelations so that the marginal changes can be evaluated; and, secondly, a precise understanding of the constraints and policies that determine the country's development both now and in the future, and hence the existing or projected circumstances in which the marginal changes will occur. "[3]

iii) The difficulties of social cost-benefit analysis

a) The definition of equilibrium prices: Shadow prices are no longer defined as the equilibrium prices that would prevail in a distribution-free economy.[4] They ... "are determined by the interaction of the fundamental policy objectives and the basic resource availabilities. "[5] Thus the calculation of shadow prices implies that there exists an intrinsic value for inputs and outputs (for a given welfare function and resource basis) and that this intrinsic value can be determined. Some authors[6] contest the existence of such intrinsic values or, if they accept their existence, consider that it is impossible to determine those values with any precision.

b) The definition of a welfare function: The process of shadow pricing presupposes "a well defined social welfare function, expressed

1.   J.M.D. Little and J.A. Mirrlees, op. cit., pp. 143-144.

2.   Squire, van der Tak, op. cit., p. 26.

3.   Ibid, p. 49.

4.   Ibid, p. 26.

5.   Ibid, p. 16.

6.   See in particular: Charles Prou: "Back to the Shadow Prices", Paper submitted to the "Colloque sur l'analyse des projets de développement," Clermont-Ferrand, 12-13 November 1973. If we admit that there is nothing like "intrinsic values" or, as a young teacher from the Sussex University said in a recent meeting organised by the IBRD in Paris, the single honest shadow prices approach is the one previously described - i.e. a set of shadow prices worked out by a central team using a mathematical programme. At this time, this simply does not exist, even in France or in the States." (p. 6).

as a mathematical statement of the country's objectives ... "[1] However, as discussed earlier, there exists no objective development function: objectives and their relative weights cannot be determined objectively. The definition of a welfare function thus depends on the characteristics of those making the valuation. There exists, therefore, not one welfare function but as many as there are different value sets represented in the society. Since shadow prices used in social cost-benefit analysis depend on the welfare function chosen, there are as many shadow prices as there are value sets represented in the society. Therefore, social cost-benefit analysis does not provide an unambiguous, unique criterion for project appraisal.

The difficulties connected with the definition of a welfare function are not specific to social cost-benefit analysis: those problems are intrinsic to project appraisal/evaluation and they will arise with any methodology chosen. Nevertheless, the existence of those difficulties explain why social cost-benefit analysis - though undoubtedly analytically the most appealing and coherent methodology - might not necessarily be the most appropriate methodology for project appraisal:

- The calculation of shadow prices (though recognised by the theoretician to depend on value-loaded preference functions) has for the user of the methodology (the decision-maker) an aspect of objectivity that is not justified.
- The language of social cost-benefit analysis and the relatively complicated and abstract concepts it uses hampers the dialogue between technicians and decision-makers.

The exactitude of the shadow prices depends on how well the technician translates the subjective welfare function of the decision-makers. On the other hand, the decision-maker can only appreciate the value of the social cost-benefit analysis if he understands the different factors that have been taken into account in calculating the various costs and benefits. Social cost-benefit analysis therefore requests a close dialogue between decision-makers and technicians.

---

1. Squire, van der Tak, op. cit., p. 49.

Little and Mirrlees, op. cit., consider quantification as a desirable goal ... "We think that as much as possible should be quantified by rule. A programme of 'discovering' decision-makers' valuations by analysing actual investment decisions is probably a wild goose chase." (p. 134/135). However, they do not consider the clear definition of a welfare function as a precondition for social cost-benefit analysis: "However, project planning and evaluation will continue to be done in many countries without the benefit of the kind of planning framework sketched above ... But this does not imply that cost-benefit analysis is useless if it has to be done without the benefit of the central government's guesses as to the future development of the economy ... Finally, social cost-benefit analysis can proceed without the analyst having explicit guidance on values. In that event, he has to be guided partly by his own sense of morality, while also interpreting government policy in a broad sense so that he does not feed in values that are at variance with it." (p. 89).

The inclusion of different objectives into one figure, however, does not facilitate this dialogue. The shadow wage rate, for example, includes in one figure four different values: the economic efficiency cost (the opportunity cost of labour), the valuation of leisure (reservation wage), the valuation of additional present consumption compared to future consumption (inter-temporal distribution) and the valuation of additional consumption according to the agent who receives it (inter-personal distribution). There are probably few decision-makers (in less developed countries and developed countries alike) who have the necessary time and understanding of social cost-benefit analysis to evaluate the implications of the calculations presented to him by the technician.

c) The goal hierarchy proposed: Social cost-benefit analysis assumes that all objectives of the Government can be expressed in two fundamental goals: "Countries have many objectives, such as better health services and more efficient agriculture, but such objectives are really means to attain more fundamental objectives that usually relate to the distribution of consumption, both over time and at a point of time. It is these two aspects of consumption - that is, its inter-temporal and inter-personal distribution - which form the basis of the welfare function employed here."[1] Not everybody would agree that all Government objectives can be reduced to those two fundamental objectives. However, even if we accept that Government objectives can be expressed in those two fundamental goals, we do not know how they relate and what they contribute to these goals. As discussed earlier, we do not have the theoretical and empirical bases for determining the relationship between various goal levels. The authors of social cost-benefit analysis admit the difficulty when discussing the value of public income: "In practice, however, it is unlikely that the Government can secure the equality at the margin of the value of additional expenditure for all purposes, especially because the value of additional expenditure in such sectors as health, defence and administration is notoriously difficult to assess."[2] Thus the reduction of Government objectives to the two basic goals is fraught with difficulties and "benefit-cost analysis may rest on conceptualisations and theories of unknown qualities."[3] Thus at the present stage of knowledge of the development function a single figure to express the benefits of a project is not enough and the revelation of the costs and benefits of a project in relation to each objective may be more informative and a better tool for decision-makers, though analytically less appealing.

---

1. Squire, van der Tak, op. cit., p. 50.
2. Ibid, p. 68.
3. Peter H. Rossi and Sonia R. Wright: "Evaluation Research: An Assessment of Current Theory, Practice and Politics", UNESCO paper, September 1976, not published (p. 50).

d) The determination of the effects of a project: Before putting a value on costs and benefits of a project, we have to identify the effects the project has on its environment: "In order to affix dollar values to the benefits of a programme, first there has to be some evaluative evidence of what kinds and how much benefit there has been."[1] How much time one spends on the identification of effects compared to their valuation depends on what we know about the potential effects. Putting high emphasis on valuating the contribution of a project to a country's socio-economic development objectives is justified if we can predict those contributions with a reasonable degree of accuracy. If the effects of a project cannot be predicted with confidence - which is often the case with so-called social projects - the emphasis has to be shifted from the valuation of effects to their identification. In such cases, social cost-benefit analysis, which assumes that the effects of a project have been identified, may be of little interest. Social cost-benefit analysis is not in competition with the project analysis framework proposed in Chapter IV. It has to be considered as the logical extension of the evaluative framework proposed.

2. Cost effectiveness analysis

Cost effectiveness is based on the same principles as cost-benefit analysis. While, however, in cost-benefit analysis costs and benefits are measured in the same commensurable unit, cost effectiveness is used to evaluate projects for which outputs and inputs cannot be expressed in commensurable terms. Cost effectiveness is therefore the logical extension of cost-benefit analysis to projects where the goals are non-commensurable and multiple. Cost effectiveness analysis defines the efficiency of different input combinations to achieve a given goal or set of goals, if the goals are identified in an operational way so that the degree of goal achievement can be measured by a set of indicators. While cost-effectiveness analysis provides the necessary criterion to choose between alternatives to achieve a specified goal or between different degrees of goal achievement for a specified input, it provides no information about the desirability of goals. Cost-effectiveness has therefore to be preceded by a goal analysis.

3. The Prou and Chervel appraisal method

i) Origin of the method[2]

The Prou and Chervel method is based on the principles of linear programming. The use of shadow prices is rejected as the authors do

1. Carol H. Weiss: Evaluation Research: Methods of Assessing Programme Effectiveness, Prentice Hall Inc., 1972, p. 84, New Jersey.
2. Charles Prou et Marc Chervel : Etablissement des programmes en économie sous-développée, tome 3, L'étude des grappes de projets, Paris, 1970. DUNOD.

not believe that it is possible to define a price for inputs and outputs that corresponds to the intersection between resource availabilities and objectives.

The method is based on the identification of costs and benefits for the various agents in the economy by taking into account the forward and backward linkages of each investment decision. Each investment decision is taken within the environment in which it will have to live and its direct and indirect effects on that environment are made explicit.

ii)   The calculations of the costs and benefits[1]

The basis for the calculation of costs and benefits is a comparison of the economic situation in the country with and without the project. The identification of the effects of the project on the economy is based on the following steps:
- identification of the direct effects of the project, i. e. , the inputs needed and the expected outputs;
- identification of the increase in the demand for intermediate products. This is done by using input/output tables, where available, or simply by tracing out the forward and backward linkages of the investment decisions;
- an analysis of the distribution of the value added created by the project;
- an analysis of the induced effects due to the use of the new value added.

The criterion used for investment decisions is total value-added created, i. e. income. The valuation of the effects is done at market prices. The analysis provides the information necessary to take into account the income distribution effect by identifying the agents which receive the income. However, the appraisal of the income distribution effect and its relation to the value added objective is left open.

iii)   The integration of Government objectives into the calculation of costs and benefits

In a recent publication,[2] Chervel abandons the appraisal of the impact by the individual preference function of the various agents of the economy, and proposes to evaluate the projects according to their impact on the "collective optimum", i. e. the evaluation of projects "within the framework of explicitly set objectives", (p. 45). He recognises the multiple goal settings of a society and the impossibility of reducing them into a single economic function. He admits that

1.   Ministère de la Coopération, République française : "Manuel d'évaluation économique des projets - La méthode des effets", SEDES, version provisoire, août 1975.

2.   Marc Chervel : L'évaluation des projets de production en économie sous-développée : Essai de typologie des méthodes, SEDES, Paris, 1974.

project appraisal has to include the specification of objectives brought about by a discussion between technicians and politicians: Project appraisal ". . . thus is no more 'a method of evaluation' in the strict sense, but an economic analysis according to the constraints and objectives set for the economy" (p. 54).

It is important to note that Prou and Chervel consider their project analysis as part of the planning exercise. The role of the project appraisor is to identify the consequences of an investment decision and to submit to the government an analysis of the effects of alternative investments. It is then up to the Government to adjust the benefits according to its objectives (income distribution, savings, foreign exchange, etc.) and to choose a package of investments that corresponds to the existing economic, social and political constraints.

iv) The differences between social cost-benefit analysis and the effects method

The two methods arc not fundamentally different and the two analyses should give similar results provided they make the same assumptions about government objectives and socio-economic constraints.

The two methods differ on the question: how and when the adjustments to market benefits should be made:
- Social cost-benefit analysis introduces government objectives and socio-economic constraints into the valuation of factor and product prices. It is up to the project appraisor to interpret government objectives and to make explicit the trade-offs between objectives.
- The Prou and Chervel method uses market prices to determine the effects of a project and it is only at the end of the analysis that the various objectives and constraints are taken into account. In the effects method, the task of the project appraisor ends with the identification of the effects and it is up to the decision-makers to adjust the benefits according to the various objectives pursued by the government.

While social cost-benefit analysis provides guidelines of how to calculate the trade-offs between government objectives, the Prou and Chervel method leaves the integration of objectives to the subjective judgement of the decision-makers. Thus the Prou and Chervel method can be considered as a simplification of the social cost-benefit analysis. Like all simplifications, the method has advantages and disadvantages: what is lost in rigour might be won in applicability. While the method does not provide a rigorous investment criterion like social cost-benefit analysis, it might well be much closer to the way in which investment decisions are taken in reality.

4.   The impact approach to the appraisal of projects

The impact approach is used by the US Agency for International Development (AID) and by the Swedish International Development Authority (SIDA).   This method elaborates a hierarchy of objectives and tries to establish the impact of a project on the development goals of a country.   It is basically a tracer study of the benefits to link logically the immediate objective of a project (target) to the intermediate (sector objective) and to the final development goals.   The method not only determines the contribution of the project to the development goals, but also specifies under what conditions and how the project contributes to the development goal.

The USAID methodology of project appraisal consists in the ". . . establishment of a logical framework for the project which: i) defines project inputs, outputs, purpose and higher goals in measurable or objectively verifiable terms; ii) hypothesises the causal (means-end) linkage between inputs, outputs, purpose and goal; iii) articulates the assumptions (external influences and factors) which will affect the causal linkages, and iv) establishes the indicators which will permit subsequent measurements or verification of achievement of the defined outputs, purpose and goal. "[1]

The logical structure and a 5 x 5 appraisal matrix are depicted in Figure III and Figure IV.

The impact approach has the following advantages:
- it tries to make the project appraisal transparent by explicitly stating the assumptions underlying the analysis and by allowing a check on the proposed hypotheses and expected results in an ex-post analysis;
- it deals explicitly with a multitude of social goals and doesn't require the reduction of the benefits into one figure;
- it is understandable to non-scientists.   It therefore can be used as a tool to clarify the trade-offs among objectives and thus to ameliorate the decision-making process;
- it is flexible with regard to information and skills requirements: it can incorporate social cost-benefit analysis, use input-output tables and partial models.   But it can also be used with rudimentary information and skills, albeit at the cost of more hypotheses and uncertainties.

The impact approach provides the necessary framework to analyse the effects of a project on various development goals.   However, it provides us with no information on the relevance of those goals nor about the efficiency of the proposed project unless the project is

---

1.   Note by USAID submitted to OECD for the DAC meeting of Experts on Aid Evaluation, Amsterdam, 27-29 June 1973, p. 1.

Figure III. THE LOGICAL STRUCTURE OF THE IMPACT APPROACH

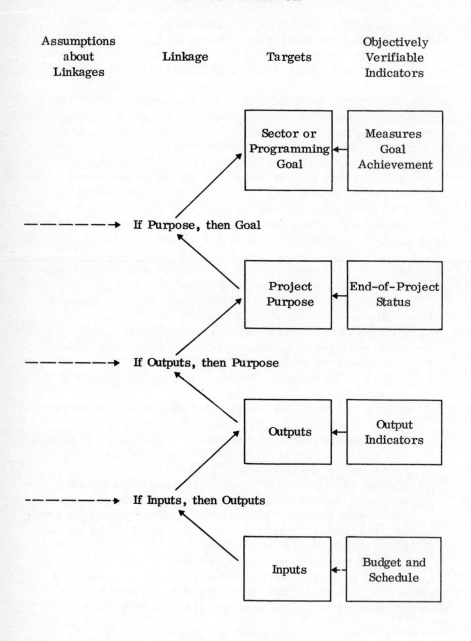

SOURCE: USAID: <u>Project Evaluation Guidelines</u>, 3rd edition, August 74, page 2, Washington.

Figure IV. LOGICAL FRAMEWORK MATRIX

Narrative summary	Objectively verifiable indicators	Targets	Means of verification	Major assumptions
Goal				
Objective				
Target				
Output				
Input				

Based on: Project Assistance Handbook 3, USAID, September 1, 1975. Appendix 3E to Chapter 3 HB3.

compared with alternative courses of action.[1] The impact approach
has therefore to be seen within a development management system that
includes goal specifications, the identification of alternatives and the
determination of feasible alternatives and their relative impact on the
goals pursued.

The different elements of such a management system are discussed
in Chapter IV.

5.   Project appraisal in reality

    i)   Decision-making theory and LDC administrations

All the appraisal methodologies discussed here are based on
classical decision-making theory, according to which decisions are
taken in the following way:
    - the analysis of a problem and the determination of objectives;
    - the identification of alternative actions available;
    - the determination of the effects of each action;
    - the use of preferences or utilities to value the different effects;
    - selection of the optimal solution.
Such a decision-making process can be applied relatively easily
when the decision involves relatively few people and when the problem
to be solved is relatively simple. For instance, a farmer can apply
this process when deciding how to manage his enterprise:
    - his problem is relatively easy to define: maximise his net
      benefit;
    - the alternatives open to him are limited in number and easily
      identified;
    - the effects of the alternative actions can be predicted with a
      reasonable degree of confidence;
    - his preference function is relatively simple and he can evaluate
      the trade-offs between objectives.
The decisions of a government which attempts to manage the
development of a whole society is not so simple: the problems are not
clearly identified; there exist an unlimited number of alternative
actions; the consequences of a decision cannot be easily foreseen and
there are as many preference functions as there are members of the
society.

There are two principal means to simplify a complex problem
solving process: [2]

1.   USAID, Handbook 3, addresses the need to integrate planning and project appraisal:
"Definition of the problems to be solved is the first step ... Subsequently alternative courses
of action will be considered as possible solutions to the problems and eventually a preferred
alternative will be selected", see Chapter 3, p. 2, op. cit.
2.   This part of the paper is based on: Lars-Erik Birgegard The Project Selection Process in
Developing Countries, a study of the public investment project selection process in Kenya,
Zambia, Tanzania. The Economic Research Institute, Stockholm School of Economics,
Stockholm, 1975, p. 35 ff.

a) Factorisation and sequential choice: A complex problem can be made manageable by decomposing the problem into its elements or sub-problems and by addressing each sub-problem in a sequential way, e. g. the health problem can be decomposed into the major health hazards and then each sickness can be treated by itself. An administrator does just that by splitting up the "government" into various ministries and directorates, each one of them with responsibility for a specific sub-problem. The decomposition of a problem into its various components is only justified if the components are seen within a hierarchical structure of means-ends relationships. This is not the case in an administrative structure: government agencies have their own dynamics and the structure of a government is rarely problem oriented. This absence of a causal relationship has important implications on project appraisal, as decisions can no longer be evaluated in a sequential way. Each project appraisal has to redefine the problem and attempt to identify alternatives, not only at the project but also at the sectoral and planning level.

b) Simplification by omissions: Omission is probably the most frequent way of simplification. Simplification by omission means that less alternative courses of action are considered. Omissions are made, intentionally or unintentionally, at various decision levels: at the level of objective definition, the determination of a strategy, programme, and at the project level. Most decision-makers are looking for satisfying solutions to a problem rather than for optimising solutions. Once the decision-maker is satisfied that the decision constitutes a step forward, he stops considering alternatives.

How many alternatives a decision-maker is willing to take into consideration obviously depends on the time and information available and on the capacity of the institution to analyse the alternatives. The particular characteristics of government institutions in LDCs do not favour the consideration of a large number of alternatives:

- LDC governments are not built up as development management institutions. Most LDC administrations are based on the
  initial colonial structure which was not set up to administer
  development but to maintain law and order. Thus the structure
  of LDC government is often not adapted to the development
  functions they are supposed to fulfil. Moreover, the tasks for
  which a government is responsible have mushroomed and
  staffing has not kept pace - especially in terms of specialised
  skills - with the diversity of responsibilities brought upon the
  government.
- The urgency of development problems puts a high pressure on
  government officials to process a large number of projects
  and to implement projects rather than to analyse them.
- Analysis is time and skill-consuming, both in scarce supply in
  LDC administrations.

45

- Information is not easily accessible and thus restricts the
    possibilities of analysis.
Thus it is not surprising that few alternatives are considered by
LDC decision-makers and that the methodology used to analyse projects
is very simple.

ii)   The project selection process

The following findings on project selection (based on case studies
in Kenya, Tanzania and Zambia) can be considered as representative
of the project selection process in most African countries and many
LDCs in other parts of the world. [1]
- The inadequate planning capacity did not allow the considera-
    tion of alternative problems. "Problem identification was
    made with almost no exception at the commodity objective
    level. " (p. 123).
- Research for alternative programmes was found to be very
    limited.
- Only one design of each project was formulated and pursued
    throughout the maturation process.
- Only one project (in Kenya) underwent changes in basic
    characteristics due to the calculation of profitability.
- Projects passed the decision points after maturation one by
    one and they were considered on their own merits without
    comparison involving ranking with other projects.
- Techniques used were qualitative and verbal in the early phases.
    More complex techniques were only used to analyse one project,
    i. e. the one finally chosen.
- Command in project appraisal techniques was very low, even
    with expatriate advisors.

iii) Consequences for project appraisal methodologies

The project selection process has the following consequences
for project appraisal methodologies:

a)   The major decisions on alternatives are taken very early in
the project planning cycle when the problems are identified and
project ideas are formulated.   It is thus necessary that project
appraisal criteria be used at the very beginning of the project planning
exercise.

b)   The search for significant problems and the identification
of alternatives constitute the most important part of a project selection
exercise.

---

1.   Lars-Erik Birgegard, op. cit., pp. 121-160.

c) Time considerations and organisational structure play an important role in the project selection exercise.

For these reasons the proposed management approach puts heavy emphasis on the analysis of the problems and the identification of alternatives (see next Chapter).

IV

SELECTED ANNOTATED REFERENCES

The books and articles referenced here have been chosen:
- for their relevance to the concepts discussed in this part;
- for their assumed availability in a large number of countries.

It has been attempted to provide some compromise between more theoretical and more practical references.

A. INTRODUCTION

1. Wilcox, Leslie D. Ralph et al.

    Social Indicators and Societal Monitoring: An Annotated Bibliography, 446 p. Elsevier Publishing Co. Amsterdam, 1972.

    A bibliography containing 1,118 listings of which over 600 are annotated. The introduction contains a review of the social indicator movement and discusses the new approach to development.

2. Wilcox, Leslie D. et al.

    Toward an Integrated Social Information System, Iowa State University, Ames, Iowa; Report No. 3, 1974.

    The authors discuss the need for information in social fields and propose an operationally feasible and society specific methodology to information gathering.

3. Nancy Baster ed.

    Measuring Development: The Role and Adequacy of Development Indicators, Frank Cass, London, 1972.

    The author addresses the problem of multi-dimensionality of the concept of development. Development is not only changes in quantity of output, but also changes in structure and institutions. A discussion about development indicators is in reality a discussion about development theory and planning.

4. Bertram Gross

"The State of the Nation: Social Systems Accounting" in
Raymond A. Bauer ed., Social Indicators MIT Press, Cambridge,
1967, pp. 154-271.

Gross proposes an information framework based on a social
system "model" including states of a nation, the system's structure and the system's performance which is useful to order some
of the information necessary in social sectors.

5. UN Economic and Social Council
Commission for Social Development, 24th Session, 6-24th
January, 1975, item 6.

Report on Unified Approach to Development Analysis and Planning,
New York, 1975.

The report analyses the shortcomings of present development
strategies. Importance is given to diagnosis and capacitation. The
report considers that, within a unified approach, the problem of
project evaluation is similar to that of derivation of objectives and
targets.

B. DEFINITIONS

1. A. Papandreou, Uri Zohar

National Planning and Socio-Economic Priorities, a two volumed
series, Praeger Publishers, 1974.

Both volumes discuss the issues of project and programmes in a
very clear and detailed way.

2. Stefan A. Musto

Evaluierung sozialer Entwicklungsprojekte, Deutsches Institut
für Entwicklungspolitik, Berlin, 1972.

The author discusses in Chapter IV the unit of evaluation and the
boundaries of the sphere of investigation. Evaluation for different
levels of decision-making are discussed.

3. USAID

Evaluation Handbook, second edition, Washington D. C. , May 1974.

This manual gives a clear description of different levels of goals
and their interrelationship.

4. USAID

The Logical Framework: Modifications based on Experience, Washington, November 1973.

This pamphlet provides a very succinct description of the goal hierarchy proposed by USAID and provides a proposal and examples for eight modifications.

C. PLANNING, PROJECT SELECTION, APPRAISAL AND EVALUATION

1. Jan Tinbergen

"Economic Policy: Principles and Design", North Holland Publishing Company, Amsterdam, 1956.

This by now classical treaty of the logic of economic policy discusses problems related to inconsistencies in individual and collective aims and proposes a decision-making model, which is useful for policies other than economies.

2. Hartmut Schneider

"National Objectives and Project Appraisal in Developing Countries", OCDE, Paris, 1974.

The author discusses the various appraisal methodologies in terms of their ability to link the projects to the national objectives. He concludes that conventional project appraisal is weak as an instrument for pursuing national objectives.

3. Andréas G. Papandreou and Uri Zohar

"National Planning and Socio-Economic Priorities, Vol. I: Project Selection for National Plans", Praeger Publishers, 1974.

The authors address the question of relating projects to national plans. They propose a structured information system for planners consisting of social trajectories expressed in vectors containing as variables so-called socially relevant indicators. An abstract rule for programme selection is given.

4. Richard V. Bernhart et al.

"Preliminary Design of an Evaluation Methodology beyond the Specific Project Level", Report to USAID, General Research Corporation, Virginia, 1975.

This report attempts to show the feasibility of goal level evaluation within a specific decision-making process.

D. PROJECT APPRAISAL METHODOLOGIES

a) Social Cost-Benefit Analysis:

1. J. M. D. Little and J. A. Mirrlees

"Project Appraisal and Planning for Developing Countries",
Heineman Educational Books, London, 1974.

This publication is a successor to the OECD publication: "Manual
of Industrial Project Analysis in Developing Countries", 1968.
The new publication includes the insights gained since the first
publication. In particular the link between appraisal and planning
is discussed and more emphasis is given to income distribution.

2. UNIDO

"Guidelines for Project Evaluation", Project Formulation and
Evaluation Series, No. 2, United Nations, New York, 1972.

The UNIDO guidelines follow essentially the same approach as the
Little and Mirrlees first Manual. However, they give to the
project appraisal and planning authority different roles. "National
parameters" (discount rate, etc.) are fixed by the planning
authority and given to project appraisors. Objectives other than
growth of future consumption are taken into account.

3. Lyn Squire and Herman G. van der Tak

"Economic Analysis of Projects", A World Bank Research
Publication, The John Hopkins University Press, Baltimore, 1975.

The S/T Method is based on the Little and Mirrlees approach.
The new method attempts to include systematically income
distributional questions into the cost and benefit stream of projects.
The calculations of various distributional parameters is discussed
in a systematic way.

4. Deepak Lal

"Methods of Project Analysis: A Review", World Bank Staff
Occasional Paper No. 16, 1974. Major cost-benefit analysis methods currently in use are discussed. The author claims - and
proves with numeral examples - that the differences in the calculations by the various methods are only due to different assumptions
and that the methods proposed are very similar as they are all
based on the same theoretical welfare economies framework.

5. Bulletin of Oxford University Institute of Economics and Statistic

   Symposium on Little-Mirrlees Manual of Industrial Project Analysis in Developing Countries, Vol. 34, No. 1, February 1972.

   The whole bulletin is devoted to a discussion of the L/M Method as published in 1968 by OECD. The different authors criticise assumptions, methodology and provide experiences with applications of the method. The bulletin closes with a response of the author to the various critics.

   b)   The Effects Method:

6. Charles Prou et Marc Chevrel

   "Etablissement des programmes en économie sous-développée, tome 3, "L'étude des grappes de projet", Paris 1970.

   This publication explains the basic principles on which the effects method is based and shows how the effects of various projects can be identified.

7. Marc Chevrel

   "L'évaluation des projets de production en économie sous-développée: Essai de typologie des méthodes"

   The principles of the various evaluation methods are given and their similarities and differences exposed. The author insists on the need to do appraisal within a planning exercise. Specification of objectives requires a discussion between technicians and politicians.

   c)   Aid Agency Manuals:

1. USAID

   "Evaluation Handbook", May 1974, Washington.

   Evaluation is designed to assist management to obtain reasonably objective information about projects and programmes in a regular fashion. The Handbook describes the AID evaluation system and discusses problems of measurement, data collection and analysis. The basis of the evaluation is the logical framework, and the three underlying criteria are effectiveness, efficiency and significance.

2. USAID

   Project Assistance, Handbook 3, Washington, September 1975.

   The Handbook sets forth the substantive and procedure role of AID in relation to projects supported by AID from project creation through the completion of the project. The Handbook gives an overview of AID project process, presents information on requirements for analysis, authorisation, monitoring and evaluation. It provides AID formats for standard project agreements and basic standard implementation documents.

3. Ministry of Overseas Development, United Kingdom

"A Guide to Project Appraisal in Developing Countries", 1972.

The Guide is based on the Little and Mirrlees method. Importance is given to the identification of a project and to the determination of alternatives. Importance of screening at all stages is stressed.

The valuation is based on the principle that in LDCs prices do not reflect the social cost of factors. The Guide describes short-cuts to derive shadow prices.

4. SIDA

"Manual of Support Preparation", Swedish International Development Agency, Stockholm, 1973.

Swedish aid is based on plans, priorities, objectives, sector strategies, sector analysis and country programmes. The initiative has to come from the less developed countries themselves. The Manual is based on a hierarchy of objectives and on the concept of in-built, on-going evaluation. Special attention is given to the concept of target groups.

5. Marc Chevrel, Michel Legall

"Méthodologie de la planification"

"Manuel d'évaluation économique des projets : La méthode des effets".

Ministère de la Coopération, République française, Paris, 1976.

This Manual is based on the concepts worked out by Prou and Chevrel. Project appraisal is seen within the framework of development planning. The authors insist on the interelationships of the project cycle and expose the various means to trace the effects of a project on the economic environment. The Manual discusses problems of integrating multiple goals and the importance of various institutional and political aspects for evaluation methodologies.

6. OECD

Aid Evaluation - The Experience of Members of the Development Assistance Committee and of International Organisations, Paris, 1975.

The report, based on an OECD meeting on evaluation, provides a concise overview of the experiences of the major donors with their evaluation efforts.

7. Lars-Erik Birgegard

"The Project Selection Process in Kenya, Zambia, Tanzania".

The Economic Research Institute, Stockholm Schools of Economics, Stockholm, 1975.

The book provides an interesting analysis of how projects are related in reality.   The author insists on the necessity of introducing appraisal criteria very early in the project identification stage and considers the formal appraisal as window dressing.

8. Hayes, Samuel, P. Jr.

"Evaluating Development Projects", Technology and Society Series, 2nd edition revised, UNESCO, Paris, 1966.

This publication, a revised edition of the "Measuring the Results of Development Projects", published in 1958, describes techniques which could be used to determine the effectiveness of projects. The publication insists on the necessity to design evaluation at the beginning of the project and suggests ways of collecting, processing and analysing data.

Part II

A MANAGEMENT APPROACH
TO DEVELOPMENT ACTIVITIES

I

INTRODUCTION

The approach to project selection proposed in this Chapter considers project appraisal as one element of an integrated information system for development management.

The management approach attempts to outline:
- the various levels of analysis required, their information needs and their respective product;
- how each element of the information system has to be organically linked to the other elements;
- how appraisal relates to planning and evaluation.

The discussion of the management approach does not imply that the appraisal methodologies discussed earlier do not recognise the necessity to link project appraisal to the planning and evaluation stage. For instance, Squire and van der Tak warn that "the use of shadow prices reflecting basic policy objectives and resource constraints only in the final stage of appraisal, when most of the essential choices have already been made, tends to be mainly cosmetic. To be an effective aid in decision-making, shadow prices should also be used in framing sector strategies and in identifying promising project possibilities and designing their major features" [1].

In the same way, the USAID Handbook 3 discusses the need for problem identification and the development of alternatives in its chapter on preliminary considerations in project formulation [2]. The management approach simply attempts to outline those different steps and to show that what is important is the analysis and not the appraisal methodology chosen. As a matter of fact, a project appraisal exercise based on the information collected during the different steps should provide the same result irrespective of the methodology chosen to appreciate the project, provided that each analysis makes the same assumption about objectives and constraints. Thus the proposed framework is not in competition with the methodologies outlined earlier, but has to be considered as complementary to any specific appraisal methodology.

---

1. Lyn Squire and H. van der Tak, op. cit., p. 18.
2. "Project Assistance, Handbook 3", USAID, 1st September 1975, pp. 3.1-3.6. See also Appendix 3 A for means-ends analysis.

A project appraisal framework is useful and used only if the following conditions are met:
- it is adapted to the social development framework of a country,
  i.e. if it addresses the relevant questions brought up in a society;
- it respects the social planning, analysis and monitoring framework of a country, i.e. if it is adapted to the organisational and
  decision-making structure of a country.

As each country has its own development path based on its values
and resources, and as each country has a specific institutional framework to analyse, define and monitor development, the project appraisal
methodology has to be adapted to each country. Since analytical models
are not defined in abstracto, but are constructed to the specifications
required by socially determined goals and by the socially recognised
feasible instruments, it is not possible to identify a generally applicable
management procedure [1]. Therefore the management approach outlined
here does not provide a predetermined specific methodology but a general
information framework for development management that can, and has
to, be adapted to the specific requirements of the various countries.

Before discussing the different elements in a project management
system, it is necessary to discuss two basic concepts:
- the project cycle and the process of iteration;
- the use of social indicators to structure the information collected
  at the various levels of analysis.

---

1. The dilemma of project appraisal manuals is due to the specificity of country and project
situations. Either the manuals are very precise and they cannot be applied to a given situation,
or the manuals are general and are too vague to be called "manuals".

II

THE PROJECT CYCLE

As discussed earlier, the different stages in the life of a project are interdependent. The output of a planning exercise becomes an input to programme planning and programme data provide the necessary information for a planning exercise. Plans need information on projects and projects need information from plans, just as project appraisal needs information from project evaluation and project evaluation requires good project appraisal. The absence of relevant information and the subjective character of the information available are the major problems a decision-maker faces when appreciating alternative actions. The uncertainty in project appraisal is primarily due to:
- the absence of an objective development functions;
- the absence of a theory of social development;
- the lack of factual information (or its incompleteness) on the social trajectory of a country;

Therefore, project appraisal has to be done:
- without the objective criteria to evaluate the goals pursued;
- with only limited knowledge of the social trajectory and its development through time;
- using largely subjective criteria to determine alternative feasible trajectories the country could pursue;
- using imperfect models to determine the effects of policy interventions on the social trajectory.

Any project appraisal methodology, therefore, relies on a multitude of implicit or explicit hypotheses about the society and its development goals to evaluate the effects of a project.

The iterative project appraisal approach (as depicted in Figure V) considers planning, policy formulation, policy execution and evaluation as an inter-related, circular search process that provides continuously new information on the social development process and thus ameliorates the decision-making process and policy execution alike.

Thus, within the management approach, project appraisal goes beyond the traditional goal of evaluating the benefits and costs of a specific project and becomes a management tool, not only for the execution of a particular project, but also for the monitoring of social policy and decision-making in general. The utility of a project appraisal methodology can therefore not be evaluated within the context of one project. For a specific project, the gains in information through the use of a

59

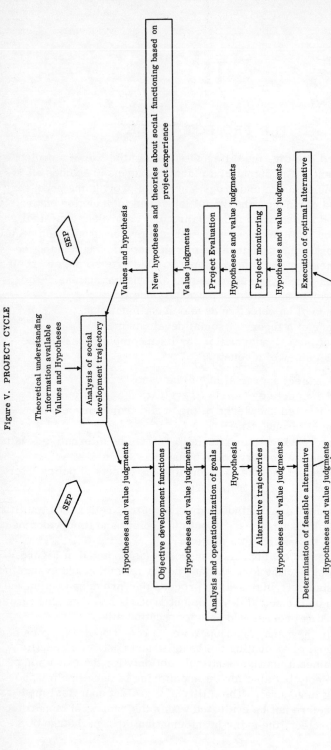

Figure V. PROJECT CYCLE

SEP = social economic political factors

NOTE: Only hypothesis is employed if there is no choice involved, only value judgment if there is only choice involved.

project appraisal methodology might be inferior to the costs inherent in the application of the method. However, the gains of project appraisal might considerably increase when seen within the general social management framework.

The iterative impact approach to project appraisal is so designed as to maximise the utilisation of the information gained by project appraisal/execution/evaluation for the amelioration of the understanding of the social fabrics and to develop a more and more efficient development management system. Thus the value of the management system is determined by its usefulness to the decision-maker. As Joseph S. Wholey points out "... if evaluation wants to survive, it is necessary to have answers to the questions of decision makers and not the questions that interest the evaluator".[1]

<hr>

1. Policy Science, Vol. 3, No. 3, September 1972: "What can we actually get from programme evaluation?", p. 362 ff.

III

SOCIAL INDICATORS
AS ELEMENTS OF AN INFORMATION SYSTEM

An integrated management approach to project appraisal requires information not only on economic variables but also on social ones. The experiences over the last two decades have clearly shown that economic statistics are not sufficient to describe the state of the society and that economic analysis is too narrowly based to explain development and to be sufficient as a tool for policy makers. It became apparent that the information base had to be broader and that social variables could not be ignored if the policies were to achieve the goals pursued. Social indicators are supposed to provide the necessary information in the social fields.

However, there exists no readily available theory to define and construct social indicators: [1]

- The development of social indicators has been characterised by the absence of a conceptual framework. Social indicators did not grow out of the operationalisation of a general social theory but were constructed on an ad-hoc basis to respond to specific demands for information. For this reason, each author tailored the concept of social indicators to his specific needs. The result is a confusion about the nature of social indicators, their use and their necessary characteristics.

- Social indicators measure only those social phenomena which the authors consider worth measuring. Social indicators (or at least most of them) are therefore not value-free.

- Social indicators have been constructed at various levels of abstraction and generalisation (local level measurement, international comparison, measurement of social services, measurement of achievement motivations, etc.).

Thus it is not possible to define in abstracto the meaning of social indicators and their characteristics. As R. V. Horn says: "... the meaning of social indicators and how one can use them are not inherent in the social indicators themselves. Those questions concern those who do the analysis, establish the plans and interpret the results. It

---

1. The author discusses the origins of the social indicator movement and the various approaches taken to measuring social phenomena in a Development Centre Working Paper, "Social Indicators and Information Needs for Policy Making", OECD Paris, May 1977.

is the users who have to know how to choose, elaborate and use appropriate indicators".[1]

1. The use of social indicators within a management system for development activities

Within an integrated project appraisal approach, social indicators are used as a means to provide the decision maker with the necessary information for the execution of his task. Social indicators are therefore used at different levels of abstraction:
- to depict the social trajectory of a country;
- to determine national objectives of social development;
- to analyse and operationalise the development goals;
- to determine alternative feasible trajectories;
- to determine the optimal alternative;
- to monitor and evaluate the policy interventions.

Thus social indicators can be considered as elements of a general information system of direct interest to policy makers. The best information system would be provided by a model that would not only determine which social indicators have to be constructed, but also how they interact. Since no such model is available, it is impossible to provide objective guidelines for choosing social indicators.

2. The iterative systems approach to social indicators

The systems approach puts emphasis on inter-relationships of social phenomena rather than on individual statistics. It shifts attention from the construction of individual indicators to the determination of an inter-related information system. The iterative approach admits that social development models cannot be constructed deductively, as development is a normative concept and that the choice of social indicators is value-loaded as long as a development model does not provide objective selection criteria. Moreover, this approach recognises that it is not feasible to collect all information possible, so that the data forms the development theory, as the cost of data collection is prohibitive. A compromise between inclusiveness of all social phenomena into an information system, and the practical requirement of parsimony has to be found. This compromise will by definition be arbitrary. The cost of data collection requires the limitation of the social information to policy needs. It will be necessary to start with basic assumptions (deduced from general development theory and prone to value judgments) and to propose hypothetical relationships. This approach has the following advantages:

---

1. R. V. Horn, "Social Indicators for Development Planning and Analysis" in International Labour Review, Vol. 111, No. 6, June 1975, Geneva.

- the social systems approach shifts attention from value-loaded goals toward the formulation of policies consistent with the social trajectory of a specific country. [1]
- the recognition of the arbitrariness of the first approach keeps analysts aware of the hypothetical nature of the proposed relationships;
- the posing of hypothetical relationships provides the criterion for information gathering to prove or disprove the proposed relationships;
- the feedback from the evaluation of the policy measures based on the hypothetical relationships permits readjustment of the concepts of social development to fit more closely the observation of empirical events;
- the circular relationship between theories and empirical realities allows the increase of our knowledge of the social development of a country as a whole;
- the focus on policy questions requires that the social indicators be adapted to the decision-making process and assures that the information is of practical use;
- the approach proposed recognises the close relationship of social indicators with analysis: social indicators do not assure a good analysis. However "a judicious selection and interpretation of indicators can reveal the weakness (of the analysis) and lead to the reconsideration of premises. This interaction of analysis and indicators on the level of knowledge is important, in particular for the global planning exercise." [2]. "... Whatever else social indicators can or cannot do, the very attempt to construct them forces attention on to the enormous problems involved in resource allocation and the formation and administration of social policy." [3]

3. Definition and characteristics of social indicators

Now that the use of social indicators within the iterative approach has been defined, it is possible to propose a definition of social indicators themselves.

i) Definition of social indicators

Social indicators are the numerical expression of various measurable aspects of abstract social concepts that are used as variables and parameters within an integrated information system for decision makers. [4]

---

1. See Wilcox, op. cit., Vol. 1, p. 34 ff.
2. R. V. Horn: "Les indicateurs sociaux pour la planification et l'analyse du développement", Revue Internationale du Travail, op. cit., p. 531/532.
3. Andrew Shonfield and Stella Shaw: Social Indicators and Social Policy, Heineman Educational Books, London, 1972, p. 8.
4. See also Wilcox et al., op. cit., Vol. I, pp. 56-76.

This definition of social indicators permits the determination of the necessary characteristics of social indicators.

ii) Characteristics of social indicators

There are three general characteristics that can be deducted from the first part of the definition:

a) the proxy character: Social indicators do not stand for themselves but are a surrogate for something else. They are supposed to translate abstract social concepts into operational terms that permit analysis and monitoring of the concept. This shows the importance of the concept relating the measurable social indicator to the unmeasurable concept it is supposed to stand for. Conceptualisation, therefore, enters into the construction of social indicators. It is the proxy character which distinguishes the social indicators from social characteristics.

While all social indicators may be social statistics, not all social statistics are social indicators, e.g., number of hospital beds/thousand of population is a social statistic collected by the health ministries of most countries. This statistic might be used as an indicator to monitor the health status of a specific country. However, this statistic would only be a legitimate indicator to monitor the health status of a country if the analysis of the health sector showed:
- that the major health problems in the country can only be dealt with by curative services;
- that hospitals can successfully deal with the major health problems of the country;
- that the major constraint in providing curative services is the availability of hospital beds.

Social statistics can be considered as the raw material for the construction of social indicators. They are collected for various purposes. Social indicators are a particular application of these statistics.

b) the measurement aspect of social indicators: The use of social indicators is part of an effort to systematise information. Therefore not just any information in the social field is considered a social indicator, but only the information which can be expressed in some measurement scale which allows certain mathematical operations. This does not exclude "qualitative information" as long as this information can be expressed in some ordered scale. A phenomenon can only be measured if it is conceptually quantifiable. Social concerns are not quantifiable; however, certains aspects of them are. Social indicators therefore only measure quantifiable aspects of social concerns. The fact that an aspect of a social concern is not measurable, however, does not imply that it is not important. The exclusion of non-quantifiable aspects of a social concern risks introducing a methodological bias into the information given by social indicators.

The quantification of indicators does not mean that they can be constructed in abstracto. The quantification of social concepts has to be based on the analysis of a specific society and "has to lean on local experience".[1]

c) the value-loaded character of social indicators: Social indicators are not value-free. Value judgments enter at different levels of the construction of social indicators.[2]
- choice of indicators: The simple fact that we measure a phenomenon means that we attribute to it a certain importance. Since measurement implies a cost, we measure only those factors which we consider important. This may explain (at least partly) why we have more economic data than social ones. Economic factors have been considered as the backbone to development efforts.
- scaling of indicators: the adoption of a specific scale implies a judgment about the importance of differences within one scale, e.g., the choice of GNP as an economic indicator implied that the distribution of the GNP was not considered as very important for economic growth.
- distribution coefficient (weighting): Many social concepts cannot be expressed with one indicator. It is therefore necessary to use several indicators to measure various dimensions of the concept. The way of integrating those different measures into one index obviously implies a judgment of the importance of the different dimensions, e.g. participation in a co-operative can be expressed by the following indicators: membership, financial contribution, contribution in kind, participation in meetings, participation in elections, participation in governing bodies, etc. What importance (weight) is given to each of those indicators in establishing an index is basically a judgment and influences greatly the "value" of the index.

Since the choice of social indicators depends on the analysis of the socio-economic context and on the problem addressed, it is dangerous to generalise specific social indicators. Each social indicator "... is a little like a word in a phrase, i.e., if the word is the sign of something, the meaning of this sign can only be understood within the context of the phrase".[3]

---

1. Rolo Moltu, Jan Isaksen: "Measuring socio-economic change", Bergen, September, 1974.

2. For more details see Jan Drewnowski: "Social Indicators and Welfare Measurement: Remarks on Methodology", (Measuring Development) Nancy Baster (Ed.), London, 972, p. 85.

3. P. Verges: "La fabrication des indicateurs sociaux: usine, ou jardinage ?" : Economie et humanisme, N° 206, juillet/août, 1972, p. 20.

From the use of social indicators as variables and parameters of a social information system, the following characteristics can be deducted:

d) The indicators should be relevant: i.e. they should provide the necessary and sufficient information for policy makers and managers. Each country has its own development style and therefore needs its own method of diagnosis with specific needs of information and hence its own particular set of indicators.[1] The choice of indicators is a political act as indicators will only reveal those social concerns which they are supposed to indicate. Social indicators can be a valuable instrument to understand the social stratification and its functioning. However, "within the framework of a system the primary goal of which is the preservation of the social status quo, the social indicator cannot be anything else but an instrument to preserve this order".[2] This puts a severe limitation on the usefulness of social indicators. Its recognition, however, is a very important factor for anybody dealing with them, e.g. social indicators might identify population groups who have no access to a given service and thus lead to corrective measures. On the other hand, social indicators might be used to cover up social problems, e.g. school construction has been expanded by 50 per cent over the last 3 years; this might cover up a much more relevant indicator: the school enrollment ratio in rural areas has declined over the last three years. Both indicators might be right; however they might not both be relevant for policy making.

e) The indicators should include aggregate, structural and distributive characters of the society: The aggregate information is necessary to depict the state of development. The structural indicators will show how different factors inter-relate while the distributive indicators (individual and regional) will show why they interact the way they do, e.g. per cent of farmers who are members of a production co-operative (aggregate indicator) provides information on the development of the agricultural co-operative movement in a country. Percentage of co-operatives providing production support to industrial crops (structural indicator) shows how co-operatives relate to agricultural production (90 per cent of co-operatives are based on industrial crops, while industrial crops constitute only 25 per cent of the agricultural production). The ratio of average size of land holdings of members to the size of land-holdings of non-members (distributional indicator) shows why the co-operatives are mostly geared to the industrial crops. (The

---

1. Country specificity has been emphasized by Wilcox et al in their Thailand study: "There is limited value also in constructing detailed comprehensive lists of indicators of social development. To rigorously develop such lists would be to dictate what it is about development that must be assessed and would be, in essence, an attempt to define social development." Wilcox et al. Vol. 5, p. 68.

2. F. Saint-Pierre, Les indicateurs sociaux dans le VIème Plan in "Economie et Humanisme", No. 206, juillet/août 1972, p. 41.

co-operatives respond to the needs of their members, the better off farmers, who are more integrated into the market economy.)

f) The number of indicators should be kept as low as possible: The utility of a social indicator will depend on the marginal increase of relevant knowledge provided to the decision-maker by including the indicator into the information system, e.g. in a given situation, information on use of high yield varieties might also cover the information "access to irrigation" as everybody who uses high yield varieties also uses irrigation. Access to irrigation would thus be a redundant indicator.

g) Indicators should preferably relate to people, not things and should be real rather than monetary: This is not a requirement but a preference, based on the assumption that most social planning is done to enhance the wellbeing of the members (or some members) of a society. The problem with a monetary indicator is that it provides "the value in exchange" rather than "the value in use" of a service or product and therefore depends on the income distribution, e.g. an indicator man-month sickness/year, if available and reliable, is always preferable to a physical indicator: hospital beds/1000 of population, etc. The determination of a minimum consumption basket in physical terms provides a better base to identify the number of people living at the poverty level than a minimum income.

h) The indicators should be economical: The collection of data costs time and money, both in short supply in a decision-making process. It is therefore necessary to be resourceful and imaginative in the use of existing data sources. Information need not be ideal to be included in the information system. It is always better to have imperfect information on a relevant question than an ideal statistic for an irrelevant question. Often information may be included in the system on the basis that it is the only information available. The information system proposed and its circular approach to policy making will provide the necessary criteria for the improvement and extension of data collection and analysis.

i) The indicators should be understandable to non-scientists: They cannot be derived by scientists alone. To develop useful social indicators, a close dialogue between analysts and policy-makers is necessary. It is not only necessary that the policy-maker understands the indicator, but also he agrees about the meaning of the indicator. It is very doubtful that the policy-maker will take action on information which he considers (rightly or wrongly) inadequate to depict the problem he is concerned with.

k) Indicators should be objective: The objectivity of data is not intrinsic to the phenomenon they measure but stems from the state of development of our ways of making and expressing observations of it. "When symbols have verifiably similar meanings to all men, we call

68

the phenomenon to which the symbols refer objective".[1] However,
since social indicators are value and culture loaded, their objectivity
can only be judged within a specific social and cultural setting and within the framework in which they are used. [2] For example, if tin roofs in
a given region provide a measure of income distribution, and if other
independent observations of the income distribution (e.g. household
surveys) provide the same results, then tin roofs can be considered
as an objective indicator of income distribution in that region.

4.   Possible errors in social indicators

Social indicators have to be scrutinised carefully before they are
used. There are three major sources of error:
- inadequate basic data: the measurement of social aspects which
are a symbol (indicator) of a larger social concept is often not reliable.
This is a problem of gathering social statistics.
- deficient link between indicator and concept: The social indicator is simply not indicating what it is supposed to. The associations
between indicator and concept might be wrongly:
a) subsumed;
b) explicitly stated, or
c) ignored [3].
For example, the possession of tin roofs might depend on climatic conditions or on the access to the raw material. In such cases, the asso-
ciation between the indicator "tin roofs" and the concept "distribution
of wealth" would be wrongly subsumed.
- deficient manipulation of social indicators: There are many
more possibilities of errors in the use of social indicators, such as

---

1.   Albert B. Biedeman: "Social Indicators and Goals", in Raymond A. Bauer: Social
Indicators", p. 134, MIT Press, Cambridge, 1967.
2.   It is often argued that physical (objective) indicators are not sufficient, as the final goal
of a planning exercise is to enhance the wellbeing of the members of a society. However,
the subjective wellbeing of a society is a function, not only of the amounts of goods and
services at its disposal, but, as Yeh points out, "the subjective economic wellbeing is a
function of the material conditions of the people compared to their aspirations, needs or to
what they deem to be entitled to (p. 9, op. cit.). It is undoubtedly true that subjective
indicators are conceptually more interesting than objective ones. However, subjective
indicators are extremely difficult to interpret and very costly to collect. Moreover, it must
be said that, while material indicators might not be very relevant to indicate the wellbeing
of the population in the rich countries, the problem is different in LDCs where a large pro-
portion of the population cannot satisfy its basic material needs. (For the treatment of
subjective versus objective indicators, see "Subjective Elements of Well-being", OECD,
Paris, 1974.).
3.   Ramkrishna Mukherjee: "The Construction of Social Indicators", in The Use of Socio-
economic Indicators in Development Planning, UNESCO, Paris, 1976, p. 39.

the ones due to the manipulation, extrapolation and the construction of composite indices. The possibility of such errors has to be checked at the level of the different uses made of social indicators.

5. A taxonomy of social indicators

The iterative impact approach as described in Figure V provides the following classification of social indicators:
- social analysis indicators: are included to depict the social trajectory pursued by the country.
- social needs indicators will provide the yardsticks necessary for the diagnosis and the determination of goals.
- goals analysis indicators include all indicators that are used to transform general development goals into operational objectives that can be analysed.
- policy indicators include all manipulative variables in the social trajectory that can become instruments for the policy-maker to achieve alternative trajectories.
- impact indicators are used to monitor the effects of the project and policies including:
  - intended impact or those transformations of the social trajectory that have been pursued by the policy intervention;
  - unintended impact or side effects, i.e. those transformations of the social trajectory that have not been anticipated or not actively pursued. They can be positive or negative.
  - the distribution of the impact if distribution is a development goal.

IV

THE DIFFERENT LEVELS OF ANALYSIS

The proposed management framework considers project appraisal as part of an analytical exercise comprising:

1. The analysis of the social trajectory

Before the decision-maker determines goals and policies he has to have information on the state of the society and a minimal understanding of its functioning. The state of society or the social trajectory can be defined "in terms of the values assumed by the variables that appear in the model employed".[1] In an integrated approach to the development analysis, the model will include economic variables such as consumption, investment, employment but also such non-economic variables as defence, pollution and self-reliance.

The problem in determining the social trajectory is one of collecting information and structuring it so as to determine the inter-relationships among social, economic, political and behavioural variables. Unfortunately, there exists no social model that gives us firm guidelines in regard to the scope and nature of information to be develop to meet the needs of social analysis.[2] There exist some techniques such as factor analysis or correspondence points, however, as Singer and Reynolds point out, "the outcome obviously is determined by which set of indicators is put up for analysis and attempts at impartiality by including large numbers of indices in the original set of data only prejudices the final set of indicators chosen".[3]

At the beginning of social analysis, the determination of the social trajectory will be very rudimentary. However, since it is only a first approximation of the social reality, what might be as important as the degree of reality and completeness of the depicted social trajectory is that it be expressed in retraceable terms and that it provide assumptions that can be tested and used to refine our understanding of the social trajectory.

---

1. See footnote 1, Part I, Chapter II, point i), p. 22.
2. The problem of what to include in the analysis of the social trajectory is obviously the same as the problem of choosing relevant indicators (see Part II, Chapter III).
3. H.W. Singer and Stuart D. Reynolds: "Aspect of the Distribution of Income and Wealth, Kenya" in The Use of Socio-Economic Indicators in Development Planning, op. cit., p. 162.

The analysis of the social trajectory should provide:

i) a description of the social trajectory: To determine realistic goals, it is necessary to understand the base line situation. The availability of data and its potential utility for analysis is much greater than generally believed. There is normally more information available than can be used. A data glut is as harmful to good policy making as a data gap. To assure the relevance of the information collected, it is necessary to scrutinise critically each piece of information to answer the following questions:
- what is the reliability of the information;
- what does the information reveal that is not already contained in other information;
- what will be the use made of the information;
- will the user utilise the information.

An empirical, statistical analysis of the information is therefore not sufficient. It is necessary to have some idea of the objectives to determine which data should be collected and analysed.

It is important to note that the social trajectory is a dynamic concept not a static one. Since planning is interested in the future, it is necessary to have some information about the expected development of the most important factors. The following analytical steps have to be executed. [1]

- selection of relevant socio-economic conditions: It is not necessary (nor desirable) to analyse all socio-economic conditions but only those which have strong ramifications with respect to various social concerns and for which there is reason to believe that their trend will change over the years.
- review of past trends: Information should be gathered on those conditions over the past years to identify the trend of the conditions and possible changes in that trend.
- prediction of future levels: Based on the trends discovered during the past, some projections should be made about the future development. Possible reasons that might influence or change the trend have to be identified.

ii) Analysis of the resources available: The purpose of the management system is to identify problems and possible actions to solve them. It is therefore necessary to have a clear picture of the resource situation. An analysis of the means available to intervene in the social development includes the following steps:
- determination of resources available: past; present; future;
- analysis of the use of those resources;
- identification of possibilities to increase future resources.

---

1. J. Bainbridge and S. Sapirie: Health Project Management: A manual of procedure for formulating and implementing health projects, pp. 65-67, WHO, Geneva, 1974.

The resource analysis should include:

- an analysis of financial resources which depend on the foreseen growth of income and the ability of the Government to mobilise those resources.

- an analysis of the basic technology options available: what is the capacity of the production system (economic and social) and what are the technologies available to increase that capacity?

- an analysis of institutional and organisational capacity: What is the Government's capacity to intervene in the various sectors and what skills can be mobilised?

2.   A first approximation of social objectives

The information gathered during the first step of the analysis, i.e.:
- information on social trajectory;
- information on resource availability;
provide the necessary information to:
       - determine the major problems;
       - to fix realistic development goals.
However, while it is possible to describe the state of development by using social indicators, it is not possible to define at which level of development each indicator should be: "The absence of an analytical conceptualisation of social development deprives those concerned of the possibility of setting up analytical goals".[1] The goal setting and the relative weight given to different goals will have to be necessarily a political choice. Some help to fix goals methodologically has been proposed:

i) comparison with a development profile: Different authors using a number of different methods have established - on the basis of international comparison - development profiles which indicate the "average" or "normal" levels of development of different sectors which correspond to each other. The distance of the country profile to the "normal" development profile would give the weight which could be attached to different goals: however, the normal profile is not the ideal profile and there may exist specific conditions in a country which justify the difference in levels observed. ·"That the profiles can only be a first approximation is shown by the fact that a relatively underdevelopped sector of, let's say, the social domain has not necessarily to be a development bottleneck".[2] International comparison can therefore

1.   Stephen H. K. Yeh: "The Use of Social Indicators in Development Planning" in "The Use of Socio-Economic Indicators in Development Planning", op. cit., p. 61-69.

2.   H. Bokerman: "Sozio-ökonomische Kriterien als Masstab für den relativen Entwicklungsstand von Länder und Sektoren, dargestellt am Beispiel Lateinamerikas" in Deutsches Institut für Wirtschaftsforschung Sonderheft 99, 1974, p. 34. The author shows that according to development profiles, Chile should have developed much quicker than Mexico, which evidently wasn't the case.

only be used with the greatest caution to specify and weight goals.

ii) Identification of a "minimum basket": The state of development can be compared with minimal standards in different social and economic fields. However, minimal standards are not easy to define objectively.[1]

Levels of minimum standards of life have to be defined politically within the cultural setting of a specific country as the definition of a poverty line (i.e. minimum conditions for a decent life) depends on the societal perception of the needs and the possibilities to satisfy those basic needs.[2] Moreover, an aggregate measure will not be sufficient and it is necessary to "define the population having permanent access to that basket."[3]

The product of this step of the analysis should be:
- an identification of the major problems and their relative importance;
- a first approximation of the development goals that should be achieved and the time frame within which they can reasonably be expected to be fulfilled.

3. Goals analysis and operationalisation of goals

The political decision-makers provide the definition of general goals of development expressed in qualitative terms.[4] The function of the goals analysis is to clarify the meaning of the development goals by decomposing the general goals into operational objectives that are useful for policy-making, and by determining the relative importance of various goals. The goals analysis thus requires a close dialogue between politicians providing the basic values and technicians who attempt to interpret the basic values and to express them in measurable terms.

i) Multiple goals analysis: Societies always pursue many relevant goals. To formulate a coherent set of policies, it is necessary to integrate various economic, political and social goals. Goals can be complementary, conflicting or indifferent to each other. Some goal conflicts are based on inconsistencies that are the consequence of

---

1. For more details see local level analysis p. 66.

2. "While basic needs which progress must satisfy may be considered universal, the nature of minima may depend on circumstances", from "The Measurement of Real Progress at Local Level", UNRISD, Report No. 73.3, Geneva 1973, p. 5.

3. Juan Sourouilla: "The Organisation of Information for Development Appraisal", UN Economic and Social Council, September 1974, New York, p. 36.

4. For the problems of identification of goals when goal setting is done at different levels of decision-making, see Musto's goal matrix, op. cit., pp. 115-122.

74

imperfections in the human mind.[1]   However, other conflicts are real...
"as a rule there seems to exist some sort of conflict between most
objectives in the sense that the fulfilment of one objective hampers to a
certain extent the fulfilment of another objective. Very often, the reason for such a conflict is the existence of a financial or physical constraints."[2] The objective of multiple goals analysis is to make explicit
the integration of various goals and to determine the trade-offs between
them. Not all goals have the same importance for the decision-maker.
Decision-makers should consider all goals and make their preferences
clear. However, for political reasons, the decision-makers do not like
to make their preferences explicit. "What is needed is a methodology
that does not require explicit intervention by the political decision-
makers, yet makes use of value judgments that must come from them
alone."[3]

The iterative impact approach to project appraisal does just that.
By determining the impact of a project on each development goal, and
by identifying values of weights that make a difference in the project
choice, it makes sure that the decision-maker is aware of the relevant
alternatives and the trade-offs involved among multiple goals. Such a
procedure, applied to all decisions, would reveal the implicit trade-offs
of the decision makers and will permit, through time, the anticipation
of the weights attached to various goals more and more precisely.[4]

The integrated approach also recognises "... that conflicts very
often cannot be harmonised in selecting investment alternatives in an
isolated way, with or without the use of weights and constraints, but
only within a balanced package of measures which reflect the relative
importance of the various objectives. Then the package as a whole
represents the compromise reached between conflicting objectives,
and the single projects contained in the package are no longer justified
exclusively on their own but to some extent as part of a bargain".[5]
Thus project appraisal has to evaluate a project as part of an investment budget, rather than as an isolated decision.

   ii) The operationalisation of goals: The analysis of the social
trajectory and the definition of the objective development function

---

1.   See J. Tinbergen: Economic Policy: Principles and Design, 1964, pp. 18-21, op. cit.
2.   Hartmut Schneider: National Objectives and Project Appraisal in Developing Countries,
OECD Development Centre, 1975, p. 10, Paris.
3.   "Planning for Multiple Goals", by Daniel P. Loucks in Charles Blitzer, Peter B. Clark,
Lance Taylor: Economy-wide Models and Development Planning, p. 33, Oxford University
Press, London, 1975.
4.   This does not assume a constant weight for each objective over time as the anticipated
weights will be based on marginal and not average utility of achieving one more unit of a
specific objective.
5.   H. Schneider, op. cit., pp. 21-22.

identify the development problems and define the general goals of development and their relative importance.[1] Unfortunately it is not possible to express those general development goals in sufficiently operational terms. Moreover, there are no methodological tools for the operationalisation of these goals and for the measurement of goal achievement. The operationalisation of goals tries to establish a hierarchy of goals and to express general development goals in operational terms that are useful in the appraisal of projects. It provides the project appraisal exercise with the necessary conceptual link between operational project objectives and development goals. While it is mostly not possible to express final aims in quantitative terms, it is possible to define the relation of operational objectives to the general development goals and therefore to derive relative weights for the operational objectives. The operationalisation of goals is the reformulation of development goals so that they fulfill the requirements of verification of goal attainment.

An example of a partial specification of goals based on the 5th 5-year Plan of India is depicted in Figure VI. The operationalisation of goals implies the decomposition of general qualitative goals into a bundle of sub-goals at a lower level of abstraction. The different objectives can then be grouped according to the instrument-goal relationship between goals of different levels of abstraction.

However, the link instrument-goal between different levels of abstraction is not a mathematical but an assumed one. Our appreciation of the link depends on our understanding of the functioning of the social trajectory and its reaction to the public intervention. It will thus depend on the analytical framework and values cherished by the analyst. Only the explicit statement of the underlying hypotheses permits the improvement of the understanding of the mean-goal relationship over time.

As Figure VII shows, the analyses at different levels of abstraction are interdependent. Goals and objectives cannot be defined and operationalised in abstracto: they depend on the analysis of the needs and the means to fulfill the identified needs.

iii) Goals operationalisation and alternative investment strategies: Goals can only be defined and operationalised in relation to an assessment of the resources available. The goals analysis thus includes an assessment of alternative policy strategies, based on the resource

---

1.   The interaction technicians-politicians is twofold:
- the technicians analyse the social trajectory and identify the options open to the society;
- the politicians provide the general goals based on an assessment of the social trajectory;
- the technicians identify the consequences of those goals and thus help to clarify them.

Figure VI

PARTIAL SPECIFICATION OF GOALS, OBJECTIVES, MEANS AND ALTERNATIVES,
BASED ON THE Vth 5-YEAR PLAN OF INDIA

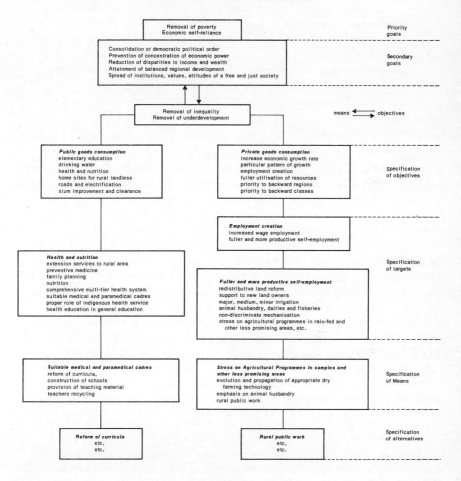

availability. Thus the goals analysis will permit the identification of the contribution of various sectors to the solution of the problems chosen and their relative importance for the achievement of the various goals.

iv) The output of the goals analysis: The analyses undertaken so far will produce the following information:
- a long-term development plan identifying the most important problems, resource availability and goals to be achieved;
- a conceptual link between development goals and various sectoral objectives;
- an assessment of various policy strategies and the relative importance of various sectors;
- an overall resource allocation between sectors.

4. The sectoral analysis

Sectoral analysis is an integrated analysis of a given sector that provides the necessary information for the formulation of a Government programme that includes an investment strategy leading to the identification of promising projects. The sectoral analysis provides the factual information necessary to clarify objectives and to evaluate the different means. The approach taken towards sector analysis is again iterative. What is needed is not a one-time all-out effort of analysis but "... an institutionalised, continuing process of analysis which can provide an informed and analytical basis for the definition of objectives, consideration of alternative policies and strategies, programme development, course correction, policy and strategy revision, and redefinition of objectives. [1] Thus the first analysis might be rather rudimentary, based on existing data. Since a gradual approach to precision is taken, it is better to have a cursory analysis that states assumed relationships and determines the data necessary to prove or disprove the proposed relationships, than to wait until means and time are available for an in-depth analysis. It is more searching analysis rather than general comprehensive surveys that is needed.

i) Definition of sector: Certain sectors are relatively easy to delineate as their main purposes are easy to analyse. This is not the case in social sectors. Social sectors are all means and no end. Their end or justification is found outside the sector, i.e., in the assessment of the needs of a particular country. Before deciding what sort of basic needs should be fulfilled by a social service, it is necessary to examine the specific environment and to identify the basic needs already satisfied and how they are fulfilled. Therefore, the delineation of the sector analysis should be related to the objectives to be accomplished. A

---

1. Intercountry Evaluation of Agriculture Sector Programmes, Colombia, Costa Rica, Guatemala, Vol. 1, June 1974, AID, p. 3, Bureau of Latin America.

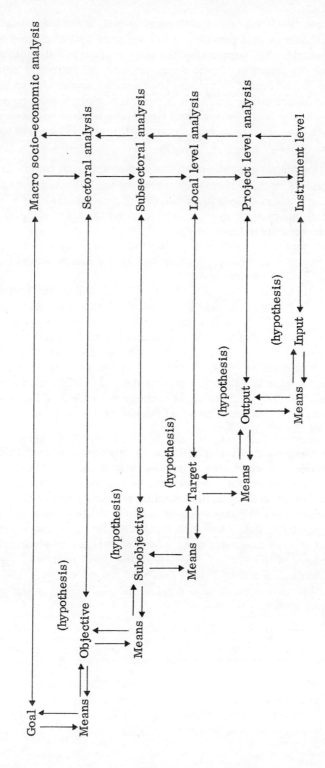

Figure VII. MEANS–GOAL SELECTION, INTERDEPENDENCE ANALYSIS – GOAL SPECIFICATION

sector thus is a complex of delineated social activities related to a specific objective and considered to constitute an "analytical entity". [1] The boundaries of a sector are therefore a matter of definition and depend on the identification of the necessary and sufficient relationships that have to be treated to analyse the "sector" in relation to its objective. To be useful for policy analysis the segment chosen must have a "relative independence", i.e., "events and conditions have to be more critically dependent upon factors operating from within than from outside the entity analysed". [2]

ii) Descriptive analysis: Before deciding what to do and how to intervene in a sector, the policy maker needs to have some information on the sector. The goal of the descriptive analysis is to set up a structured information system to determine the level of development of the sector and its functioning.

Stock indicators: They describe the sectoral situation, its inputs and outputs in very much the same way as the macro analysis, but at a different level of abstraction.

Structural indicators provide the information on the production process and its performance at the sectoral and subsectoral level.

Indicators of inter-sectoral dependence: Sector analysis is a partial analysis. Though it is hoped that the delineation of the sector has been done in such a way that it embraces the critical relationships necessary to understand the functioning of the sector, the environment in which a sector is set cannot be ignored. To define the functional relationship among sectors, it is necessary to identify the most important inputs from other sectors and the use of sectoral outputs in other sectors of the society.

iii) Diagnosis: Diagnosis is the "analytical approach that examines the specific characteristics of development within the framework of a system of inter-relations, within and between the sectors". [3] Each sector consists of a "system of social, political, economic and technological resources, linkages and products". This system defines and determines the quantity and distribution of the goods and services produced. [4] The diagnosis is supposed to assess the structure and performance of the sector. To assess the performance of a sector, it is necessary to compare it with some reference values. The reference level chosen will very much depend on the philosophy and understanding of the development process.

---

1. Intercountry Evaluation Agriculture Sector Programmes, op. cit., p. 12.
2. Ibid.
3. "Report on Unified Approach to Development Analysis and Planning", UN Economic and Social Council, 24th Session, 6-24 January 1975, item 6, p. 4.
4. US AID: "The Methodology for assessing rural development projects: a project statement". May, 1975, p. 5, Washington.

iv) Criteria to evaluate the performance of social sectors [1]

a) Efficiency of the sector performance. The efficiency of a service can be approximately established by determining the relationship between output and input. However, it is not possible to establish sectoral capital coefficients. It will be necessary to evaluate the efficiency according to the specific constraints under which the sector is working. A comparison with some standard be it planned efficiency, efficiency in other countries, regions or sectors will have to be made.

b) Relevance: The analysis of relevance of a social service refers to the broader purposes that are pursued by the society. It therefore requires determination of the contribution of the social service to the goals analysed earlier. For this it is necessary to understand the functioning of the society and to determine the inter-relationships between the service and other factors influencing the goal achievement. The relationship purpose-objective is not a mathematical, but a conceptual link and identifies the information needed to check the validity of the proposed link.

c) Coverage: The criterion of coverage, as used here, is not a general criterion, but relates to a specific objective. It is assumed that general access to social services is a development goal. Because of the ubiquity of this goal, the coverage criterion has been included. The criterion of coverage here is not used to determine how and why certain people have access to social services and others not. The disaggregated analysis of efficiency and relevance has provided that information. The criterion of coverage is supposed to evaluate the feasibility of expanding existing social services or proposed new ones to cover the total population in the country that is in need of the service. A health service might be very efficient and relevant, as long as it is limited to a pilot area. Its extension over the whole country might, however, be impossible with the given (material, financial, human, organisational) resource constraints. The criterion forces the analyst to adapt the quality of the service provided to the resources available. The need for quality staff and management has to be critically evaluated, if show piece and enclave projects are to be avoided.[2]

---

1. For a step-by-step analysis of efficiency, access and relevance of an educational sector analysis, see Brandon Robinson: "A Methodology for Education Sector Analysis", US AID, Bureau of Latin America, 1975.
2. The criterion of coverage addresses the problem of replicability of the service provided to the total population in need of that service. The criterion is very important for the evaluation of social services where regional disparities (in needs and services provided) are very important. The enquiry into the capacity should include an assessment of socio-cultural feasibility of the interventions. For a discussion of an approach to "social soundness analysis, see: Project Assistance Handbook 3, USAID, op. cit., Chapter 5, App. A, pp. 1-12.

v) Disaggregation of data: An aggregated efficiency, relevance and distribution level does not identify where and how the efficiency, relevance and distribution could be increased. The information has thus to be disaggregated according to suspected differences in the levels:

Regional disaggregation: A health system might be very efficient and provide a good coverage in an easily accessible, heavily populated plain, but inefficient and providing access only to the lucky few in a mountainous sparsely populated region. An education system might be very relevant for an urban population, but not correspond at all to the needs of the rural population.

Occupational disaggregation: The problems of coverage for a health system are different according to various occupations: it is to be expected that the coverage level of the same health system would not be the same for nomadic herders, farmers, industrial labour or white collar employees.

Income level disaggregation: A health education project (hygiene) would have a different relevance/efficiency for a well-to-do audience living in quarters supplied with running water than for poor families having only contaminated water at their disposal.

Disaggregation according to assets: The command of assets (land, know-how, political access, health) will determine whether a target group will be able to take advantage of a proposed opportunity or not.

Disaggregation according to type of economy: A credit system for the modern industrial sector or for commercial farming will differ in its efficiency, relevance and coverage from a credit system for the informal urban sector or the large traditional agricultural sector.

Disaggregation according to social (tribal) classes: The relevance and coverage of a project will vary according to the different beliefs and traditions connected with a particular activity or service.

The disaggregations proposed are neither complete nor exhaustive.[1] The disaggregations chosen will depend on the particularities revealed by the local level analysis and on our understanding of the importance of given particularities. While the disaggregation may be relatively arbitrary in the first analysis, the iterative approach will allow a gradual move towards greater precision.

The analysis of the different efficiencies, relevances and coverages (compared, if available, with data on other countries or regions similar to the country studies) will allow the determination of a yardstick and to identify (in a first approximation) the factors influencing the efficiency, relevance or coverage of the sectoral output:

- factors due to insufficient resources (financial or manpower),
- factors due to administrative and organisational shortcomings,

---

1. It is not sufficient to find a measure of dispersion as we need to know which social groups benefit or not by the output. See Juan Sourouilla: "The Organisation of Information for Development Appraisal", UN, Economic and Social Council, 26th September, 1974, New York.

- factors due to misunderstanding of the problem the service is supposed to solve or about the social setting within which the programme is working.

vi) Output of "sectoral analysis": Such a sectoral analysis should provide:
- a disaggregated picture of the social trajectory at the sectoral level,
- a first assessment of the efficiency of the sector,
- a first assessment of the possibility to provide access to everybody,
- a first assessment of the relevance of the sector activities, according to the objective pursued,
- a first identification of factors that could increase efficiency relevance and access,
- a first assessment of resources available,
- a first listing of alternative social trajectories available (disaggregated into target groups and regions),
- the identification of means to achieve alternative social trajectories,
- the assessment of the financial, social, political and organisational feasibility of the means available,[1]
- the identification of a feasible set of policies and activities to achieve a more desirable social trajectory,
- the evaluation of feasible alternative solutions and the selection of an optimal action programme,
- a clear statement of the hypothesis utilised and an identification of data needed to validate or invalidate the hypothesis,
- a plan for the collection of data for the next sectoral analysis.

5. The local level or micro-analysis

The sectoral analysis may determine the functioning of the sector and identify its problems. However, it will only indicate a situation, the explanation of which will have to be found through analysis at the micro-level. While the sectoral analysis will indicate the problems, the solutions to those problems will have to be found at a local level. The information needed at the micro-level can be divided into:

i) Information on needs: Defining the basic needs of the population is essential for the determination of the objectives pursued by policy interventions. Real (non-monetary) indicators can be used to determine the level of satisfaction of basic needs and to determine the areas that need intervention to increase the level of satisfaction of those needs.

---

1. "... we have to work hard and imaginatively at designing and redesigning possible courses of action. Whatever the scope of the problems that is initially chosen, the design of alternatives to be evaluated is a vital aspect of analysis." McKean, op. cit., p. 54.

To determine the level of satisfaction of basic needs, it is necessary to choose a yardstick of minimum standard of living. Unfortunately, it seems impossible to establish normative needs scientifically. The minimum standard of living will therefore have to be determined according to the social setting of the country concerned. The determination of a minimum standard of living cannot be divorced from traditions, general expectations, the capacities of the country, and there will always be some "moral" element in it.[1] The demand of goods and services (or the willingness to pay) cannot be taken as a measurement of social needs in a society where a large part of the people live in the subsistence sector or where the existing income distribution is not considered as the desirable one. "Vast need and potential demand for basic consumption goods on part of low income masses of population do not get registered in the market; the effective demand therefore reflects the prevailing structure of income distribution".[2] It will thus be necessary to determine physical minima of consumption in different fields that are considered the necessary conditions for a decent life, however this might be defined in the given society. In reality for most countries in the Third World this means to define minima for nutrition, housing, clothing, health, education and working conditions. Once the consumption in these fields are known and disaggregated according to the relevant social and geographic stratification of the society, it should be possible to define a rational consumption basket for the country that takes into account physical consumption norms, consumption reality, possibility to increase consumption and the social perception of consumption needs.[3]

The present low level of information on the consumption of specific goods and services (especially the lack of disaggregated data according socially relevant population groups) might not allow the identification of a rational consumption basket for a given country. In that case, it might be possible to disaggregate consumption baskets according to regions and sectors and to determine norms based on the criterion of reduction of sectoral and regional disparities. The drawback of a geographic or sectoral definition of needs is that any region or sector includes some whose needs are already satisfied. As mentioned in a seminar on development projects designed to reach the lowest income groups, this "might in fact be a desirable feature of development projects", at it is necessary for successful project implementation "to

---

1. The simplest way of analysing the needs at the local level would be to base the analysis on the needs expressed by the people. However, there is a "close relationship between the degree of politicisation and the willingness and ability of rural people to articulate their demands for social services" (Uma Lélé, op. cit., p. 100 ff). Thus the expression of needs might reflect more the political power structure at the local level than the real needs of the mass of the population.

2. "Report on Unified Approach to Development Analysis and Planning", UN Economic and Social Council, 24th Session, 6-24 January 1975, item 6, p. 4.

3. The needs analysis is based on Schwefel, op. cit., pp. 9-18.

compromise with the existing power structures", and thus to recognise "the impossibility of limiting projects uniquely to the lowest income groups".[1]

While such an approach is hardly attractive for the scientist, a minimum basket of physical consumption so defined has certain qualities that are essential if the minimum basket has to be used in decision-making and planning:

- it assures that the minimum basket is politically and socially acceptable;
- it assures that the minimum consumption basket is not a theoretical ideal, but an operational concept adapted to the physical and socio-economic conditions of the country;
- it permits the identification of the poor by comparing the national consumption budget with the actual class-specific consumption budgets and provides information about the goods and services required by the mass of population;
- it provides the necessary raw material to establish priorities and thus to determine a hierarchy of objectives at the sectoral and macro level;
- the value-loaded and specific character of the minimum consumption basket recognises the hypothetical character of any basket and the need to redefine the basket in a continuous analytical search for better understanding of the social trajectory of the given country.

ii) Information on capacities: Real[2] indicators should reveal the potentialities and constraints to satisfy the basic needs defined earlier. The capacity indicators will define the limits of intervention and allow the determination of the feasibility of alternative interventions proposed. The capacity study should reveal the natural resources endowment of the area concerned (region, village, quarter), the commercial capacities (access to markets and inputs), the technical capabilities (level of technical know-how) and the political institutional capacities (social structure, interest groups, administrative abilities).

The analysis of local capacities is very often limited to the determination of constraints. However, for the identification of alternative actions it is more important to determine what exists than what is lacking. This is particularly important if we attempt to find solutions that are adapted to the local situation. Thus, for instance, an understanding of the traditional health services available (traditional midwives, healers, labour related to hygiene, etc.) might open up many alternative approaches to improve the health situation that are more efficient and better adapted to the local situation than the classical approach of constructing a health centre.

---

1. OECD Development Centre: "Seminar on development projects designed to reach the lowest income groups", Paris, 17-19 June 1974, Summary and conclusions, p.3, mimeo, 1975.

2. "Real" means indicators expressed in physical terms rather than monetary indicators.

iii) Response indicators: These indicators should provide an answer to the question, "Who could reasonably be expected to participate?"[1] They should provide information on the attitudes of the people towards modernisation (tribal society, traditional community partly affected by modernising influences, communities in transition). While subjective indicators would be the ideal, because of conceptual difficulties and the necessity for the indicators th be cheap, replicable and easily available, it will be necessary to use objective indicators such as use of modern inputs, radios, traditional or modern authority, etc. It will be necessary to elaborate a detailed typology for ordering communities according to their responsiveness.

iv) Distribution indicators: The needs, capacities and responses are not uniform, even at the local level. It is therefore necessary to disaggregate provincial data on needs, capacities and responses according to identified cleavages into village and household data. It should be possible to determine at the local level, a set of specific assets and relationships that would be representative of the distribution of needs, capacities and response at the local level. As UNRISD asserts "at the village level therefore, one can find real data, without extensive income or expenditure surveys, that describe aspects of distribution and, in particular, participation in development of lower castes and classes".[2] If primacy is given to man's needs and potential, one "... must question prevailing social structures and the position and way of life of those groups which, intentionally or not, are involved in maintaining those structures".[3]

The local level analysis should provide a set of alternative projects with quantifiable targets which:
- respond to the needs of the people,
- are adapted to the local resources situation,
- are adapted to the level of modernisation of the people concerned,
- take explicitly into account distributional considerations.

v) Characteristics of social indicators at the local level: Indicators at the local level for project evaluation appraisal can be specific to the problem and people of the area studied, as they need not be aggregated. They will have to be cheap, i.e., available or easily obtainable. As they are supposed to describe the local situation, they will have to be defined and constructed at the local level. Their validity depends on the fact whether the constituent variables (indicators) represent the contingent variable, i.e., the local situation correctly. Their relevance depends on the fact whether or not the indicators define the

1. AID project System, April 1975, USAID, Washington.
2. Wolf Scott et al, "The Measurement of Real Progress at Local Level. Examples from literature and a pilot study", UNESCO, Report No. 73.3, Geneva 1973, p. 13.
3. Joost Muitenbrouwer, "Some reflections on necessity and feasibility of a unified approach" ISS Occasional Paper, The Hague, August 1974, No. 46, p. 13.

Figure VIII. THE INTEGRATION OF ANALYSES AND THEIR INTERDEPENDENCE

LEVELS OF ABSTRACTION		DIAGNOSTIC INDICATORS (QUANTITATIVE OR QUALITATIVE)	TARGET INDICATORS (QUANTITATIVE)
macro-analysis	Definition of goals	Macro socio-economic indicators	Not quantifiable
	Weighting of goals	Descriptive analysis of inter-relationships: Explicit statement of major assumptions.	Weights (1–100) of different development goals.
	Definition of sectoral contributions to different development goals	Descriptive explanation of contribution of different sectors to general goals achievement. Explicit statement of major assumptions underlying relation sector-goal.	Weighting (% contribution) of each sector to achievement of development goal.
sectoral analysis	Operationalization of sectoral objectives.	Explanation of derivation of quantitative sub-sector objective.	Quantitative target of sub-sector objective to be achieved.
	Weighting of sectoral objective	Description analysis of contribution of specific target subobjective to achievement of sectoral objective.	Hierarchy of sectoral objectives. Weighting of subsectoral objectives (% of contribution).
		Link: macro-micro analysis	
	Weighting and choosing projects	Qualitative explanation of relation project target – sectoral objective. Explicit statement of major assumptions.	Hierarchy of projects defined at local level by using weights derived from macro analysis.
micro-analysis	Contribution of project targets to sectoral objectives		Impact indicators – contribution % of each alternative to sectoral objective.
	Definition of project targets	Establishment of quantitative targets according to inputs available and production function.	Output indicators.
	Alternative solutions to problems	Explanation of contribution of inputs to output.	Indicators of efficiency "production indicators".
	Definition of local problems	Micro-socio-economic analysis.	Local level indicators.

relationships we need to identify and appraise a project. Their sufficiency will depend on whether the indicators choosen provide all the information that is relevant to the specific problem we are facing. However, a word of caution is necessary:
- the indicators provide only the information they are supposed to, i.e., if the questions asked by the use of the indicators are irrelevant, the indicators will be useless;
- the indicators are only the manifestation of a social situation. The explanation of the particular social situation revealed, will have to come from a social analysis or sound social theory.

The iterative approach and the formulation of proposed inter-relations in verifiable terms will permit a continuous advance towards more and more precision and at the same time better and better indicators.

6. The integration of the analyses and their interdependence

The five analyses proposed:
- the analysis of the social trajectory,
- the determination of the societal objectives,
- the goals analysis and the operationalisation of goals,
- the sectoral analysis,
- the local level or micro analysis,
cannot be isolated. Each analysis depends on the output of the other analyses and provides information used by the other analyses. An iterative approach in which any new insight into one analysis provides new hypotheses for the other analyses permits progress towards a better understanding of the social fabric of a country. The total information system and its interdependence is schematised in Figure VIII.

The system described in Figure VIII provides the necessary compromise between "top down" and "bottom up" planning. Past experiences have shown that "top down" planning is too divorced from the local reality to be able to muster the necessary participation of people, without which no sustained development can be achieved. The involvement of the people concerned in the analysis of their situation is necessary if the Government has to rely on their voluntary participation on the actions planned, either because it is not willing or not able (politically or administratively) to obtain forced participation. "But just as overdoing 'top down' planning can be damaging, overdoing 'bottom up' planning may result in misallocation of scarce resources".[1] In the integrated planning system proposed, the needs and the actions to meet them are identified at the local level. "The plan (then) moves up through the system to appropriate levels of aggregation at which levels resources are allocated according to criteria known and understood by all participants." [2]

1. S.H. Butterfield: "Draft Summary Statement of a practical agency approach to rural development", USAID, February 28, 1975, Annexe K, p. 3.
2. Ibid.

V

PROJECT APPRAISAL
WITHIN A MANAGEMENT SYSTEM

Within a management system such as the one described in the preceeding pages, project appraisal becomes a manageable exercise.

The planning exercise provides the project appraiser with the following information:
- Determination of the major problem areas;
- Identification of goals and a goal matrix to relate targets to purpose, purpose to objective and objectives to final development goals;
- A consideration of alternative strategies, sector allocations and programmes and a choice between them;
- An identification of alternative projects.

Thus, the boundaries of project appraisal are clearly delimited:
- Project appraisal does not define goals and their operationalisation - a task which is anyhow impossible at the project level. The project appraiser has simply to determine the effects of the project and how they relate to the goal structure given to him.
- Project appraisal has no longer to take into account all alternatives possible and try to attempt to compare a hospital construction project with an irrigation project or an airport construction. The previous analyses will have made the necessary comparisons and allocated the resources between sectors (and between programmes within sectors) so that the project appraisal exercise is just the final phase of a decision-making process in which projects within a programme are compared.

Thus project appraisal consists of the following steps:
- Determination of expected contributions of alternatives actions to the various goals.
- The determination of costs-benefits of the various actions.
- The design of a conceptual framework to monitor and evaluate the proposed action.

This section will only discuss the first two steps. The third step will be discussed in length in Part III.

1. Determination of expected contributions of alternative actions to the various goals

In the management system, goals, objectives and purposes are not questioned at the appraisal stage: they are given by the higher level analyses. Moreover, the alternatives are limited to a few and they have been identified and justified by the higher analyses. The purpose of the project appraisal is simply to identify the optimal solution by comparing the contribution of possible actions to the chosen goals. There are three steps involved:

i) Determination of all possible actions within a programme and their expected contribution to the chosen goals

GOALS	ALTERNATIVE ACTIONS (PROJECTS)				
	(1)	(2)	(3)	(m)	(M)
Y_1	X_{11}	X_{21}	X_{31}	X_{m1}	X_{M1}
Y_2	X_{12}	X_{22}	X_{32}	X_{m2}	X_{M2}
Y_n	X_{1n}	X_{2n}	X_{3n}	X_{mn}	X_{Mn}
Y_N	X_{1N}	X_{2N}	X_{3N}	X_{mN}	X_{MN}

Y_n = goals pursued by the society.

N = number of goals pursued.

M = number of alternative actions identified.

X_{mn} = contribution of mth alternative on nth goal.

This step is necessary to assure that all actions within a programme receive due consideration and to force the appraiser to explicitly state the alternatives taken into account.

ii) Identification of a feasible set of alternatives

Out of the possible alternatives, a set of feasible alternatives[1] will be chosen according to the economic, social and political constraints. It is necessary that constraints be explicitly mentioned, and that the hypotheses for the exclusion of possible alternatives be stated, so that their appropriateness can be checked in an ex-post evaluation.

---

1. For a discussion of the concepts of feasible and dominant set of alternatives, see Papandreou and Zohar, op. cit., Vol. 1, pp. 14-32 and Vol.2, pp. 37-41.

iii) The determination of a dominant set of alternatives

Once a feasible set of alternatives has been determined it is possible to restrict the number of alternatives by determining the dominant set. An alternative is considered dominant if its contribution to each individual development goal is not inferior to the contribution of any other feasible alternative to the same goal. Thus it is only the dominant set of alternatives that will be examined further. To choose among the dominant set it would be necessary to know the preference function of the decision-makers (or of the society). However, as mentioned earlier, the preference function is rarely stated explicitly. Moreover, technical problems of transforming the different figures into one comparable scale are value-loaded. For these reasons, it is better to submit to the decision-makers the analysis disaggregated by goal rather than to construct a single index of net benefits. This does not exclude the use of weights for sensitivity analyses, such as suggested in Chapt. IV, 3. The final weight given to the various goals will not depend on the project alone; the choice will depend on the other actions taken by the Government to achieve the various goals. It is therefore necessary to evaluate the project's contribution to the various development goals within the investment package considered by the Government.

The following example on expected contributions of a set of feasible actions to various development goals portrays the operationalisation of the above mentioned three steps. It is assumed that the different phases of the management system have identified the overall goals and the following six sectoral objectives:

a) The sectoral objectives

health: increase in life expectancy at birth from 45-55 years by 1985.

nutrition: ameliorate the nutritional standards by assuring a minimal caloric coverage of 2,200 calories per person, of which at least 10 per cent from lipids, to everybody by 1986.

housing: The Government has expressed its housing goal in facilities and living space available per person: i) to provide a minimum level of dwelling space to the majority of the population by assuring an average of 2 persons/room for 90 per cent of the population, and ii) assure convenient access to safe drinking water to 80 per cent of the urban and 40 per cent of the rural population.

employment: The Government's employment goal is expressed in numbers of new jobs created. The number of jobs created/year should at least absorb the increase in the labour force. Since the growth of the estimated labour force (3,000,000) is 3,5 per cent, 105,000 new jobs will have to be created/year.

income: The Government has identified its income goal in distributive and growth terms: increase of the income of people under the average income level by 50 per cent while achieving an overall income increase of 5 per cent per year.

environment: The Government has specifically identified "environment" as one of its major concerns that should be considered in determining the benefits of a project. However, no clear definition or targets to be achieved have been identified.

b) The alternatives to be considered

The higher level analyses have determined an investment programme which includes the rice production project that is the subject of this example. Thus the project appraisal has no longer to justify this choice but attempts to determine the contribution of alternative ways of organising the project.

c) Relation between project target and sectoral objectives

It is rare that the impact of a micro project on the sectoral goals can be traced directly. It is necessary to have a clear means-goals analysis to see how the project relates to the sectoral goals. Moreover, though it is attempted to show the relationship between the overall sectoral objectives and the project, it is not possible to establish the causal link between project and development goals. The achievement of the sectoral objectives depends on numerous other factors which are independent of the project. However, this is not necessarily a problem: in project appraisal we do not attempt to see how the project in isolation relates to the sectoral objective, but how the project within the given programme, taking into account all the other actions foreseen, contributes to the achievement of the sectoral objective. It is obviously always possible that the particular project achieves its targets and that the sectoral objective is not met, or that the sectoral objective would have been met even without the fulfilment of the project target. This will show that our analysis of the situation was incorrect and thus provides the information to correct further planning. However, as long as we have no reason to believe otherwise, we assume that the fulfilment of the project target is necessary to achieve the sectoral objective and will lead to the fulfilment of the sectoral objectives if the other conditions (policies, project, etc.) are fulfilled as foreseen in the overall programme.

d) The contribution of alternative rice projects to the sectoral objectives

The effects of the alternative rice projects could be linked to the identified goals in the following way:

Health: The different types of rice production might have a different incidence on the health situation, e.g. a rice settlement scheme might enable the project to provide easy access to a health clinic to the regrouped population or permit the supply of clean water to the homesteads, while a production on disbursed small plots might not allow the taking into account of these additional services. The effect of these alternatives could be measured in "reduction of water-related diseases", reduction in numbers of deaths of children between 0-4 years, etc. The means-goals analysis will then provide the necessary information on how those micro variables relate to the sectoral goal of increasing life expectancy at birth (see Figure IX as an example).

Nutrition:[1] The increased production of rice/capita will provide a rather direct link to the sectoral goal. The different alternatives might have quite different effects on nutrition. A plantation type of project might help in terms of nutrition more to the urban poor, who will receive greater quantities of rice through increased production, rather than the relatively few cultivators.

An individual plot rice production might involve many more cultivators who are (or are not) below the minimal coverage of 2,200 calories, i.e. the sectoral objective. To determine the project's impact on the sectoral objectives, it is therefore necessary to trace the production process to the final beneficiary (see below).

The explicit consideration of all sectoral objectives (and not only the objectives directly pursued by the specific project may suggest simple ways of increasing the beneficial effects of the project. If rice is the principal staple of the cultivators involved in the project, the following simple measures could increase the nutritional benefits of the project in a significant manner:
  - the choice of semi-artisanal processing of rice, rather than an industrial process to preserve the vitamin B contained in rice;
  - the introduction of a complementary crop such as soya to provide the necessary proteins for a balanced diet.

This is why it is suggested that project appraisal explicitly investigates the possible effects of the project on all sectoral goals.

Housing: The project might have no direct effect on housing. However, it might have an indirect effect: by contributing productive employment in rural areas, the project could slow the rural-urban migration and therefore contribute to the solution of the urban slum problem.

Again, such an effect might be quite different according to the alternative chosen: a plantation type of project might be considered to uproot social ties and therefore increase migratory tendencies, while an individual plot production would avoid pressure to migrate by providing production activities in the traditional environment.

If such an effect on migration can reasonably be expected, it is necessary to estimate the number of avoided migrants. The higher level analyses will show how this number can be related to the overall sectoral goal.

Employment: The effects of alternative rice production schemes on employment might differ significantly: the plantation approach might decrease the open unemployment and create new service jobs.

---

1. Nutrition can be considered as a sub-objective of health. In this particular case, it is assumed that the Government wanted to underline the importance of nutrition by elevating it to a sectoral objective. There is no reason why this couldn't be done. However, the analyst will then have to be very careful not to double-count the effects of a project.

Figure IX. HEALTH: MEANS-END RELATIONSHIP

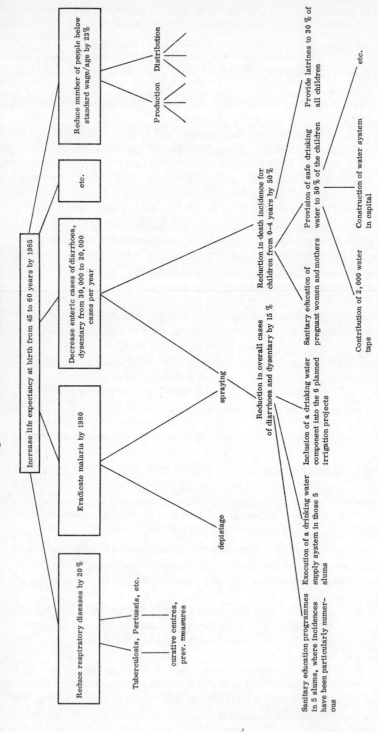

The individual plot approach might decrease only disguised and seasonal unemployment. However, more jobs may be created for the marketing (collection) of harvest and the distribution of inputs. How to value these different effects on employment will depend on the problems on the problems identified, the objectives set and other actions taken according to the higher level analyses.

Income: The income generated by the project alternatives may be expressed in additional income weighted according to the income stratification in the country. [1]

$$G = W_1 G_4 + W_2 G_2 + W_3 G_3, \ldots W_n G_n$$

G = total weighted income created by the project.

G_n = income created in each level.

W_n = social premia (+, -) on generating one unit of additional income at each income level.

n = number of differentiated income groups and number of weights attached to additional income.

The income stratification will be based on the higher level analyses and the distributional weights on the income distribution goals of the country.

Environment: The major environmental hazards defined by the country study are soil erosion and health hazards due to the creation of artificial ponds and waterways, or due to the creation of crowded living conditions. The environmental costs of crowding, water and soil erosion of the various rice production schemes have been taken into account in the determination of the effects of the projects on housing, health and value-added goals. A recalculation here would amount to double counting of the same effect. Therefore the analysis here would be limited to any particular effect not yet covered by the other objectives and would be indicated as positive (+) or negative (-).

Figure X summarises this example.

2. The determination of costs and benefits of the project

i) The determination of benefits: The benefits are defined as the difference between the social trajectory with the project, and the social trajectory without the project. The analysis of benefits therefore consists of:
- the analysis of the effect of the project output on the development goals;
- the comparison of the level of fulfillment of development goals with and without the project.

---

1. Redistribution with growth, op. cit., p. 39.

Figure X. EXPECTED CONTRIBUTIONS OF ALTERNATIVE RICE PRODUCTION PROJECTS TO VARIOUS DEVELOPMENT GOALS

GENERAL GOALS	SPECIFICATION OF GOALS	MEASUREMENTS AT PROJECT LEVEL
Health	Increase in life expectancy at birth from 45 to 55 years by 1985	Reduction of water-related diseases
Nutrition	Assure minimum coverage of 2,200 calories/person of which at least 10% from lipids to everybody by 1985	Number of people in the target group who have achieved the average nutritional level because of the project
Housing	Dwelling space of an average of 2 persons/room for 90% of the population by 1985 Convenient access to safe drinking water to 80% of urban and 40% of rural population	The number of avoided migrants The number of induced migrants Number of people who have received convenient access to safe water
Employment	Creation of 105,000 new jobs per year	Number of jobs created The number of unemployed avoided by providing remunerative activities in rural area
Value added	Overall economic growth of 5% per year Increase income of people under average income level by 50% by 1990	Additional income created weighted according to the income stratification of the country
Environment	Concern without definition	Enumeration of potential positive or negative effects on the environment

N.B. The justification of the proposed goals and measures is provided by the analysis of the specific problems the country and project are facing, e.g. the number of avoided migrants is only a good indicator:
- if the analysis shows that the housing conditions in the rural areas are better than the ones a new migrant would find in a town;
- if there is no other indicator available that measures the contribution of the project to housing in a better or more cost-effective way.

a) The direct benefits of a project are the primary contribution a project makes to the solution of an identified problem, e. g. the direct benefits of a water supply project are: a reduction in water related diseases and a reduction in the cost of water, etc.

b) Secondary effects of a project are effects which are not directly brought about by the project but which affect in one way or another the achievement of development goals. Secondary effects include externalities and multiplier effects, e. g. sanitary measures such as personal hygiene, village cleanliness, privies, etc. , seem to be impossible unless a safe and convenient water supply either preceeds or accompanies them. It is possible to identify the effects of the water supply project on other sanitary measures which might be undertaken in the region. If such effects are considered to be potentially important, it will be necessary to identify the specific effects expected and to provide guidelines for their measurement during the execution of the project.

c) The indirect impact of the project: Projects often have effects which are not intended and which do not affect the designated beneficiaries. Unfortunately it is difficult and most often impossible to foresee all the "hidden" effects of a project. However, to identify as many effects of the project as possible, it is necessary to extend the analysis from the intended beneficiaries (target group) to the environment of the project so as to determine:
- how the environment reacts to the project;
- how the project affects the environment.

To answer those questions, it is necessary to understand the functioning of the society. Thus it is important to determine what will happen, given the social setting in which the project functions, rather than to state what project appraisers want to happen.

The analysis of the indirect impact of the project tries to establish the effect of the project on the achievement of the identified goals for people living in the environment of the project but who are not direct beneficiaries of it. To determine the effects of the project on the environment, it would be necessary to compare the level of achievement of the development goals by others than the target groups in the project's environment with a control group unaffected by the project. The indirect impact can be positive or negative:
- positive: a water supply project can affect also the people who do not benefit directly from the new water source by cutting down the infecting agents that are brought into the traditional water supply system. However, spread effects of a project have to be planned for rather than assumed to occur.
- negative: a small scale irrigation scheme, though increasing substantially the income of the small farmers who are within the scheme, might affect adversely the bulk of the small farmers who, because of the location of their land or other constraints, will never have access to sufficient water for irrigation. In the

97

same way, a project, though creating employment for a substantial number of unemployed, but producing products that are not consumed locally, might increase the general price index of goods in the region and thus impoverish those who have no direct benefits of the project. The project's effects would thus be to increase the "misery of the mass of the people to the benefit of a minority of privileged workers".[1]

d) The socio-economic significance of a product: To determine the various benefits of a project, it is necessary:

- to trace the product to its final use and to establish the relation of the end use of the product to the fulfillment of the stated development goals. While this is relatively easy for a consumption good (such as rural water supply, etc.) it becomes more tedious for intermediate products: it is necessary to have some understanding of their contribution to the various final products for which they are used and of how those final products relate to development goals. An illustration of the use of a carburettor factory to the fulfillment of certain development goals is reproduced in Figure XI.

- to determine the final beneficiaries: The impact of the benefits of a project on the social trajectory is not neutral to the particular characteristics of the beneficiaries. It is therefore necessary to determine the beneficiaries of a project. The direct beneficiaries of a project are not necessarily the real beneficiaries, e.g., the experience with African agricultural development projects [2] has shown that in an agricultural production project, the real beneficiaries of the project are not the farmers but a market organisation, the state or the urban population. It is therefore necessary to trace the product to its end user and to determine who reaps the benefits of it. (For product path analysis, see below.)

The initial distribution of assets will be the major determinant of who can benefit from the project. It is clear that the benefits of infrastructure projects (road, irrigation, electrification) will be distributed proportionately (and probably even more) to the distribution of assets (land, access to technology, access to fertilizers, etc.). A grouping of households according to the types and productivity of their assets permits concentration on the causes rather than the symptoms of an existing income distribution.[3]

It is important in project appraisal not only to determine the positive impacts (i.e., benefits of a project) but all effects of the project on all the different development goals. It is not enough to know the impact of a water project on health but it has also to be determined what impact the project has on other development goals that are not

---

1. See Detlef Schwefel, op. cit., p. 37.
2. See Uma Lélé, op. cit.
3. See "Distribution with Growth", op. cit., p. 44.

necessarily intended. If a piped water project has a negative impact on employment (water carrying is an important source of revenue for many of the poorest in some countries), this impact should be identified and clearly balanced in the cost-benefit analysis.

ii) The determination of costs: The determination of costs is in no way easier than the determination of benefits. Since the demand and price structure in the country is assumed not to represent the real value of the goods and services, it is necessary to trace the impact of the withdrawal of the goods and services used in the execution of the project to the achievement of the stated development goals, just in the same way as the effects of the project had to be related to the development goals. It will therefore be necessary to undertake a "product path analysis" of each input into the project to determine its costs, measured as a negative contribution to the achievement of the development goals. This is very much the same reasoning as is behind the determination of shadow prices. The "cost" of a project input is not only determined by the relative scarcity of the input, but depends on the contribution the input would have otherwise made to the achievement of the development goals.[1] The scarcity criterion is implicit in this reasoning: if the project uses an input, that would have been unused otherwise, its "cost" will be zero, as the input, in absence of the project, would have contributed nothing to the development goals.

Example: The task is to determine the cost of cement used as an input in a health delivery project. The first step of the analysis will consist of determining what are the alternative uses of cement:

- if there is an overproduction of cement the cost of using cement in the health project will be zero;

- if cement is in short supply it will be necessary to determine whether the use of cement in the health project will lead to an increase of cement production or a diversion of the use of cement from other projects to the health project;

- if the increased demand for cement will lead to increased production the cost of cement will be equal to the cost to the society of producing the additional amount of cement;

- if the increased demand for cement will divert the use of cement from other uses to the health project, it will be necessary to determine the cost of the foregone use of cement in other sectors. To determine the foregone production of cement in other uses it is necessary to determine for what cement has been used and how this use related to

---

1. While social cost-benefit analysis aggregates the cost of withdrawing one input from the contribution it would have otherwise made to the achievement of the development goals, here it is proposed to identify the cost to each development goal separately. Social cost benefit analysis thus does the same analysis but goes one step further in aggregating the various costs into one figure.

Figure XI

PRODUCTS PATH ANALYSIS

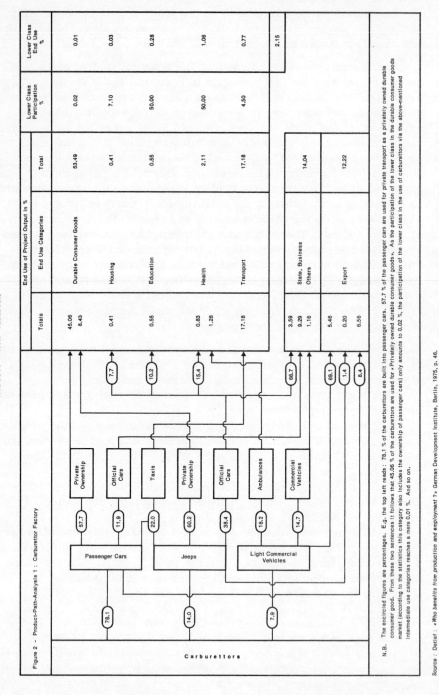

Figure 2 - Product-Path-Analysis 1 : Carburettor Factory

N.B.   The encircled figures are percentages. E.g. the top left reads : 78.1 % of the carburettors are built into passenger cars. 57.7 % of the passenger cars are used for private transport as a privately owned durable consumer good. From these two sentences it follows that 45.06 % of the carburettors are used for «Privately owned durable consumer goods». As the participation of the lower class in the durable consumer goods market (according to the statistics this category also includes the ownership of passenger cars) only amounts to 0.02 %, the participation of the lower class in the use of carburettors via the above-mentioned intermediate use categories reaches a mere 0.01 %. And so on.

Source : Detlef : «Who benefits from production and employment ?» German Development Institute, Berlin, 1975, p. 46.

the society's objectives. If the development goals are expressed in terms of sectoral objectives in housing, health, education and basic food production a product path analysis may indicate that past use of cement was distributed in the following manner:

10% for activities related to the housing objective
3% for activities related to the health objective
3% for activities related to the basic food production
5% for activities related to the education objective
79% for purposes not related to the development goals as defined in the national plan.

Knowing the importance of cement to the achievement of the above sector goals we can calculate the impact on the various sectoral goals of the withdrawal of one unit of cement for the health project.

While such an analysis might not be justified for all project inputs (the information gain might be disproportionate to the cost of information gathering), the analysis is very useful in comparing alternative procedures and different technologies to achieve the same project output (modern technology - intermediate technology).

iii) The net benefits of a project: Once the impact of all benefits and costs on the social trajectory have been determined, it will be possible to determine the contribution of the project to the development goals by establishing the expected difference between the level of development goals with and without the project.[1] The net benefits of the project will be given, disaggregated by each development goal. The trade-offs between the various development goals and their weighting will be left to the political decision-makers.

3. Two practical problems

i) The introduction of time: The costs and benefits of a project do not occur all at the same time. Moreover, it is not irrelevant to the decision-maker when the costs and benefits of a project occur. To be able to compare alternative project proposals, it is necessary to reduce the stream of benefits and costs over time to the present. There exists no specific criterion to determine the time span to be considered. McKean defines the time horizon as "the length of time over which costs and gains were estimated and beyond which one could not see well enough for estimates to be worthwhile".[2]

We assume that the time preference of the decision-maker in respect to each of the development goals can be separated from other aspects of its overall preference system[3], and thus it is possible to deal with the time preference by associating to each development goal a social discount rate.

---

1. For definition with-without project, see Part I "definitions".
2. McKean, op. cit., p. 75.
3. See Papandreou and Zohar, Vol. 1, pp. 35-40.

The determination of the various discount rates is undoubtedly difficult. The chosen value will not only depend on the resources available and the interdependence of social goals, but is basically a political choice. The problem of choosing social discount rates is abundantly treated in the literature of social cost-benefit analysis. The fact that it is not money but houses, health status, or participation that are discounted is no conceptual problem, as there is no attempt made to aggregate them.

ii) The problem of uncertainty: Uncertainty plays an important role in project appraisal for less developed countries. Many opponents of project appraisal consider uncertainties as so great that they condemn any attempt to calculate net benefits of a project as an exercise in futility.

The uncertainties in project appraisal are due to a lack of theoretical understanding of the development process and its interdependencies and a lack of data. The hypothetical character of the analyses has been stressed at all levels of analysis: opinion and subjective judgments have been entered at each step of the analysis. It is therefore necessary to introduce these subjective elements into the formal analysis of decision-making when comparing alternative action possibilities.

Uncertainties can be treated in two ways during a project appraisal exercice:

a) Uncertainties can be calculated into the benefit stream: Uncertainties can be included into the formal analysis of the benefit stream through sensitivity and risk analysis:
  - sensibility analysis changes the value of certain key variables to determine the effects of such changes on the final analysis;
  - the risk analysis uses probabilities to express the likelihood of the occurrence of the values proposed for the most important variables.

It is important to have clear ideas about the relative importance of individual variables comprising the cost-benefit stream.[1] This will allow the determination of not only the benefits hoped for and their probability, but also the probability of another outcome and the effects of the misinterpretation of the social system.

b) Uncertainties can be diminished by analysis and information gathering. By structuring the information used into a decision tree and by attributing subjective probabilities to the hypothesised outcomes, it is possible:[2]

1. For example, a farmer might refuse to introduce a new technology if there is a 9-1 chance of success as the negative outcome (crop failure) might threaten his survival.

2. The method proposed by Howard Raiffa, where it is assumed "that the decision-maker wishes to choose a strategy for experimentation and action that is logically consistent with i) his basic preferences for consequences; and ii) his basic judgments about the unknown states or events", xxiii) seems particularly adapted to the approach taken here. See Howard Raiffa: Decision Analysis: Introductory Lectures on Choices Under Uncertainty, Reading, Mass. 1968.

- to determine the value (decreased uncertainty) of more information or analysis;
- to identify which factors have to be closely monitored, i.e. the critical items which have to occur if the final benefit is to be realised.

The identification of uncertainties for the management during project execution is treated at some length in Part III.

VI

RESUME AND CONCLUSIONS

1. The management approach considers the distinction between social and economic projects as unjustified; economic and social factors are interdependent and cannot be treated in isolation. It is therefore necessary that a unified or integrated approach be taken for the appraisal of non-directly productive and directly productive projects alike.

Thus a project appraisal/evaluation team has to include economists and sociologists for economic and social projects alike.

2. The integrated approach to project appraisal requires information not only on economic variables, but also on social ones. Social indicators are supposed to provide the necessary information in the social fields.

The development of social indicators has been characterised by the absence of a conceptual framework. Social indicators did not grow out of the operationalisation of a general social theory but were constructed on an ad hoc basis to respond to specific demands for information. The result is a confusion about the nature of social indicators, their uses and their necessary characteristics.

The proposed management approach considers social indicators as variables and parameters within an integrated information system for decision-makers. It recognises the value-loaded character of social indicators. The proposed iterative approach to policy-making will permit a continuous improvement of the understanding of social development and thus allows an improvement of the choice of indicators so that they fit more closely the observation of empirical events.

The iterative systems approach to social indicators recognises that the choice of social indicators depends on the analysis of the socio-economic context and on the problematic addressed. It is therefore not possible to determine a set of generally applicable indicators, but the construction of social indicators has to bear on local experience.

The use of social indicators as variables and parameters within a management system for decision-makers permits the definition of certain necessary characteristics: social indicators have to be relevant, quantifiable, economic and understandable to non-scientists.

3. The management approach to project appraisal requires information that goes beyond the project's direct sphere. Project appraisal can therefore not be treated in isolation but has to be considered as one element of an integrated information system including:

104

- analysis of the social development of the country;
- analysis of the needs of the country;
- determination of development goals;
- determination of alternative feasible means to achieve the stated goals;
- selection of the "optimal" means to achieve the stated goals;
- execution and evaluation of the policy intervention.

Each element of the information system has to be organically linked to the other elements and the analyses have to be executed within the same framework. The macro analysis has to provide guidelines to the sectoral analysis, the sectoral analysis has not only to analyse the problems, but also to identify alternative solutions to the problems.

It is therefore necessary that a communications system be institutionalised among the agencies responsible for the various analyses.

4. The management approach puts the project back into the society. It shifts attention from project appraisal to the analysis of social development. More resources and time will have to be made available for social analyses, if project selection is to improve.

5. The approach shifts attention from the project to policy formulation: it therefore tends toward programme rather than project aid.

6. The management approach recognises that:
- the definition of an objective development function is value-loaded;
- our knowledge of the performance of a society is very rudimentary.

It therefore considers planning, policy formulation, project appraisal/execution and evaluation as an interrelated circular search process that provides continuously new information on the social development process and thus ameliorates the decision-making process and policy execution alike. This approach requires
- that projects have an experimental design, i.e., project appraisal has to formulate hypotheses and provide a design to gather the necessary information to test the hypotheses. Quasi experimental (or if possible, randomised) designs should be set up and the necessary data (including control data) should be identified.
- that the feedback from project evaluation to planning analysis be institutionalised.

VII

SELECTED ANNOTATED REFERENCES

A. SOCIAL INDICATORS

1. Nancy Baster (ed.)

    "Measuring Development: The Role and Adequacy of Development Indicators", Frank Cass, London, 1972.

    This book gives a good overview of the problems of measuring development. The author discusses three different approaches to the construction of development indicators: 1) the theoretical, deductive approach; 2) the empirical, inductive approach; and 3) the development of indicators in an operational context.

2. USAID

    Social Indicators: A Selected List of References for AID Technicians

    AID Bibliography Series, Technical Assistance Methodology No. 2, December 1972, Washington.

    This annotated bibliography is designed for the use of practitioners. A short guide identifies introductory materials, reading materials on definitions and concepts and background reading on the growth of the social indicator movement. Ninety-two items, published before April 1972, are annotated.

3. Leslie D. Wilcox et al.

    Social Systems Models of Indicators of Social Development, Iowa State University, Ames, Iowa, Report No. 1, December 1972.

    This report, based on an extensive literature research, discusses the different approaches to social indicators according to their use. The authors opt for an adaptive model in which modernisation is an evolutionary coping process. The authors take an inductive and pragmatic approach to social indicators. They propose unique models around specific development planning processes of specific nations.

4.   Andrew Shonfield and Stella Shaw (eds)

Social Indicators and Social Policy, Heineman Educational Books, London, 1972.

The book gathers contributions made for the conference on social indicators sponsored by the Social Science Research Council. The development of social indicators, problems of definitions and the need and use of social indicators for policy planning are discussed.

5.   Nations Unies

Conseil Economique et Social

"Système de Statistiques Démographiques et Sociales" (SSDS) "Projet de directives concernant les indicateurs sociaux" Commission de statistique, Genève, avril 1974.

The paper reviews the various international activities in the field of social indicators. Criteria and statistical methods for the construction of social indicators are given and the indicators proposed by OECD are compared to the indicators contained in the SSDS. A set of indicators is proposed for various social fields.

6.   Donald V. McGranaham et al.

Contents and Measurement of Socio-Economic Development: An Empirical Enquiry, UNRISD, Report No. 70/10, Geneva, 1970.

The author discusses the construction of development profiles by reducing 73 indicators to a set of 18 key variables. The development index is applied to a large number of countries.

7.   Wolf Scott et al.

The Measurement of Real Progress at Local Level: Examples from literature and a pilot study, UNRISD Report No. 73/3, Geneva, 1973.

The author examines examples of indicators derived at the local level. The author concludes that at the village level one can find real data without extensive income or expenditure surveys that describe aspects of income distribution and participation in development. A case study in Crete illustrates problems of measuring progress at the local level.

8.   N. T. Mathew

Reassessment of Real Progress at the Local Level: A contribution towards planning social and economic development in India, UNRISD Report No. 74/10, Geneva, 1974.

The author proposes a disaggregated system of progress monitoring in India, consisting of socio-economic observatories in each State and a central unit to analyse and make the statistics useful. The indicators are chosen according to their importance to planners and to the ease of collection.

9. UNESCO

"Socio-economic indicators: theories and applications"
International Social Science Journal, Vol. XXVII, No. 1, Paris, 1975

This volume contains several articles on theories and models of indicators and social change and provides some applications to regions (Asia, Africa, France, India). The papers are very candid about the limitations imposed by current planning procedures to the use of social indicator information.

B. MANAGEMENT APPROACH
AND DIFFERENT LEVEL ANALYSIS

1. J. Bainbridge and S. Sapirie

Health Project Management - A Manual of Procedures for Formulating and Implementing Health Projects, WHO, Geneva, 1974.

The Manual provides a very structured approach to the management of health projects by integrating problem identification, strategies, project formulation and implementation. The Manual proposes a logical stepwise approach to the different analyses, taking into account the specificity not only of the country, but also of its particular organisational structure.

2. USAID

"AID Project System", April 1975, USAID, Washington

This paper describes the various phases of a project from the identification document, its review, to the appraisal stage. Special attention is given to the social soundness analysis and to the identification of beneficiaries.

3. Papandreou and Zohar, op. cit.

The two volumes of these authors address the question of integration of project objectives with national goals. Particular attention is given to the identification of alternative actions to resolve an identified problem.

4. Daniel B. Loucks

"Planning for multiple goals" in Blitzer, Charles, R., Clark, Peter B., Taylor, Lance (eds):

Economy-wide models and development planning, Oxford University Press, London 1975

The author discusses the different approaches to multiple goal planning. Quantitative modelling techniques are considered to be of considerable value as aids, but not as substitutes to the responsible political decision-making process. The method proposed consists of the generation of feasible but improving plans through the active involvement of the responsible decision-maker in the planning process.

5. Hollis, Chenery et al.

"Redistribution with growth", Oxford University Press, London 1974.

The book attempts to lead the path to a theory that integrates the two goals of growth and income distribution. The book refuses a radical change in planning techniques but proposes a reorientation: an ecclectic rather than a doctrinaire approach to strategies is proposed. The authors recognise the urgency of setting relevant objectives and formal appraisal is not considered as the essence of the process. "The importance of appraisal criteria is that they provide guidance concerning the types of projects to be sought and concerning the design of projects".

6. Uma Lélé

The Design of Rural Development: Lessons from Africa, A World Bank Research Publication, the John Hopkins University Press, Baltimore and London, 1975.

The author bases her recommendations on an analysis of a variety of rural development projects. The achievement of rural development aims requires consideration of interactions among national development. The author recommends fewer but better prepared projects; a learning by doing approach, and a combination of planning based on the systematic acquisition of knowledge and flexibility in the course of implementation.

7. Peter Michael Rügner

Methodische Ansätze für die Aufstellung von mittelfristigen länderbezogenen Entwicklungshilfe Programmen, Deutsches Institut für Entwicklungspolitik, Berlin, 1972.

The book provides operational guidelines for a country approach to an aid programme. The framework includes the different levels of analysis and identifies information requirements at each level.

C. SECTORAL ANALYSIS

1. Brandon Robinson

   "On Methodology for Education Sector Analysis", Methodological Working Document, No. 53, 1975, Bureau of Latin America, USAID Washington.

   The paper stresses the need for analysis as the first logical step to planning and strategy, leading from programme or project design to implementation, evaluation and new analysis. Sector analysis is seen as a continuous process. The various steps to analyse sector performance based on the criteria of efficiency, access and relevance are outlined in a systematic way. The publication ends with a chapter on the limits of the proposed methodology.

2. USAID

   "Inter-country Evaluation of Agriculture Sector Programme" Vol. 1, Summary Report, USAID Bureau of Latin America, June 1974.

   The paper discusses the sector approach, programme content and results, as well as aid procedures and the relation to country development plans and assistance by other institutions. Based on the 3 country experience, the paper makes recommendations concerning programme content and sector analysis. The paper considers that the key to the analytical process is the building of a strong and effective analytical base from a continuing series of partial analyses.

3. M. G. Hultin

   "Guidelines for Education Sector Reviews and Education Pre-investment Study Programmes", May 1973, IBRD.

   The author briefly describes the objectives of World Bank financing in education and objectives of educational sector reviews. A strategy of education sector review is outlined, comprising six steps.

4. Russel Misheloff

Colombia health/nutrition analysis: general methodology
Health Methodological Working Document No. 34, USAID, Sector
Analysis Division, December 1973, Bureau of Latin America,
Washington.

The paper discusses the need for an analytical framework to
choose between sectors, to determine effectiveness, to judge
consistency of different policies and the feasibility of achieving
simultaneously diverse goals. To maximise access to health
services, the paper proposes to develop a spatial grid map and to
locate health facilities on that map. A central health model and
its components are discussed.

5. OECD

Seminar on Development Projects Designed to Reach the Lowest
Income Groups: Summary and Conclusions, OECD Development
Centre, Paris, August 1975.

The paper discusses target group identification, causes of impov-
erishment and different approaches to helping the lowest income
groups. The project approach and aspects of motivation and self
help are discussed. The paper concludes with some suggestions
for aid donors and for follow-up activities.

6. Hans Helmut Taake

The Implementation of Development Plans: Organisation and
Policies, German Development Institute, Berlin, 1974.

The author shifts attention from model building to goal definition
and from writing plans to their execution. He considers that with
increasing development, planning becomes less and less efficient
as uncontrollable variables and increasing internal complexities
become more and more important.

7. Riad D. Tabbarah

"The Adequacy of income: a social dimension in economic development" in "Measuring Development: Special issue on development
indicators" Journal of Development Studies, Vol. 8, No. 3,
pp. 57-76. April, 1972, London, Frank Cassel Co.

The author insists on the fact that physiological needs are not
relevant for social behaviour but that it is the socio-economic
status that defines needs. He rejects the method of purchasing
power equivalent and proposes average adequacy standards for
international comparisons.

111

8. Charles R. Blitzer

"The Status of Planning: An Overview" in Economy-wide Models and Development Planning, op. cit.

The author considers effective planning as the establishment of efficient flows of information. He proposes a set of models which together cover key issues facing the planner. In a summary of the evolution of planning techniques, the author considers thus that there is a widespread acceptance of planning techniques and of shadow pricing.

9. Janos Kornai

"Models and Policy: The Dialogue between Model-Builder and Planner" in Economy-wide Models and Development Planning, op. cit.

The author discusses the machinery of planning and mathematical model-builders. A model should be simple, taking into account the intellectual absorptive capacity of local, practical planners. It should not be imposed, but should emanate out of the planning agency itself. The opening of models to human aspects, distributional questions and to the problems of quality of life is advocated.

10. Detlef Schwefel

"Who Benefits from Production and Employment", German Development Institute, Berlin, 1975.

This book provides an operational method to determine and evaluate the benefits of projects, given the goal function of ensuring a minimum standard of living consistent with human dignity. To determine the objectives, it is necessary to identify the basic needs of the mass of the population. A comparison between a national consumption budget with actual class specific consumption budgets, the author attempts to answer the two questions: who are the poor and what is poverty? To determine the socio-economic significance of a production, the author proposes a method to determine who is the end-user of the product and does this end-use meet basic needs.

D. MANAGEMENT OF RISK AND UNCERTAINTY

1. Howard Raiffa

"Decision Analysis: Introductory Lectures on Choices under Uncertainty", Addison Wesley, Reading, Mass., 1968.

This textbook discusses the analysis of problems and the use of judgmental probability. An analytical framework to decompose more complex problems and to attach to each decision point a subjective or objective probability is given. The textbook includes a chapter on group decisions and on the cost of implementing the approach.

2.   R.E. Peterson, K.K.

"Public Administration Planning in Developing Countries: a Baysian Decision Theory Approach in Policy Science, Vol. 3, No. 3, September, 1972, p. 371.

This article elaborates in a very concise way the subjective probability decision-making theory. It treats the problem of estimations of probabilities of successful initiation and implementation of various strategies. The use of a tree-diagram putting subjective or objective probability codings at each decision point is proposed.

3.   Ward Edwards, Marcia Guttentag, Kurt Snapper

"A decision-theoric approach to evaluation research" in Elmar L. Struening, Marcia Guttentag: Handbook of Evaluation Research, Vol. 1, pp. 139-182, Beverly Hills, California, Sage Publications Inc., 1975.

The authors attempt to provide a usable, conceptual framework and methodology that links inferences about states of the world, the values of decision-makers and decisions. The article criticises current evaluation research approaches and proposes using multi-attribute utility analysis for decisions. The approach is outlined in the form of 10 analytical steps and a practical example is given.

Part III

SETTING UP A MONITORING/EVALUATION SYSTEM
FOR SOCIAL PROGRAMMES

I

INTRODUCTION

Within a programme management system as the one described in Part II of this paper project monitoring and evaluation[1] is a clearly defined management tool. The different phases of project analyses provide project management with the necessary guidelines on what and how to monitor and evaluate the project. Thus the project monitor/evaluator is provided with:

- operational definitions of the problem the social programme addresses and of the specific effects expected from the project;
- a clear logic of how the project inputs, activities and outputs relate to each other and to higher level goals;
- a detailed work plan indicating what the project is supposed to provide and how;
- an analysis of the critical elements in the project/programme which have to be monitored/evaluated;
- agreed-upon measures to determine the effects of the project;
- an analysis of the use that will be made of the information collected and of its importance in the decision-making process.

The project monitoring/evaluation will be limited to the following tasks:

- choice of the most appropriate methodology to collect the information requested;
- data collection and analysis;
- presentation of the information to the decision-makers in a policy relevant way.

However, the management system described above is an ideal that rarely, if ever, exists in a government. The iterative systems process is not going on and therefore the monitoring/evaluation cannot be part of it. The fact is, whether we like it or not, that evaluations are simply not integrated into a management system. It is therefore necessary to take a more ecclectic approach to project monitoring and evaluation. Part III of this paper thus attempts to discuss how a useful monitoring/evaluation system can be set up in the absence of the management system described in Part II.

_____

1. The term "monitoring/evaluation" is defined in Chapter III, point 1.

II

CURRENT REPORTING EVALUATION PRACTICES

In current practice "evaluation" is not considered as part of a
management approach to project execution but is an ad hoc exercise.[1]

1. Information Components of a Project

A project has normally the following information components:

i) A project document which was used to obtain the financing
of the project. A project document normally has three parts:
- a justification of the project which describes the problem in
general terms and explains why the project should be executed.
Since the project document has to receive the support of many
people, the justification will be very general, so that nobody
can disagree with it;
- a determination of the objectives. The goals of the project are
normally kept vague: improve the living conditions, make
education more relevant to the needs of the rural population,
provide better health care, etc. There is generally no agreement on what these terms really mean. Moreover, the effects
of the project are normally inflated to assure the acceptability
of the project to the decision-makers;
- a description of activities and a work plan. Normally there
exists a detailed description of the inputs which involve a
budgetary expenditure. A project document will describe how
many facilities will have to be constructed, what sort of training
will be administered, what staff (and of what qualification) will
be needed. However, how those services will be provided, and
their particular content are left to the professional know-how of
the project staff.
This project document is the basis for all future monitoring and
evaluation activities. It is evident that the value of an evaluation will

---

1. The time and content of an evaluation is very often determined outside the project or
programme management. The evaluation is often considered as a control imposed on
management. We would prefer a "conspiratory alliance" between evaluator and project/
programme management to analyse the project and to improve its management.

be influenced by the information contained in the project document, which often is the only source to determine what the project was initially supposed to be.

ii) The reporting system

Project staff is normally required to submit regular reports. These reports are considered as a control system to assure that the project is executed according to the work plan and that funds are used in the authorised way. The reports explain delays in the construction work, problems of procurement, etc. They describe the physical progress of project implementation by providing information on activities undertaken and products produced, e. g. a progress report on a health centre would provide information on how many people have been vaccinated, how many latrines installed or on how many in-patients have been treated. A project staff in charge to provide services is not going to provide information on the effects of those services.

iii) The standard evaluation

Most projects are evaluated in some way or another during their life.
- The "evaluation" mission. Very often the decision to undertake an evaluation is made when the project is in serious trouble (i. e. when the activities foreseen in the working plan are not executed), when the project is close to completion, or when a new phase of the project is foreseen. Most of the time the evaluation is limited to a few weeks. The evaluators, people not directly involved in project management, examine the project document, the files, general statistics and project reports. They undertake a visit (2-3 weeks) to the field, admire project constructions, interview project management and other government officials who are in one way or another related to the project. If they are really serious, they attempt to get some information from readily accessible project beneficiaries.

It is clear that such an evaluation has to limit its analysis to whatever information there is readily available. Since project documents and reports concentrate on inputs, activities and outputs the "evaluation" will concentrate on and analyse whether and how the project executed its tasks. Any impact evaluation if at all attempted will rely on subjective judgements that can be accepted or rejected by project management.
- The evaluation report. The evaluation report is normally written at the Headquarters in the capital, away from the project. Since the "evaluators" are often outside professionals with other obligations the final report is rarely available before 6 to 12 months after the evaluation mission. Often project management contests the evaluation report: the report does not take into account the local

situation; it does not address the questions management is interested in or has the authority to act upon or the reasoning behind the project analysis is rejected. The result is a report with management suggestions based on a subjective assessment questioned or directly opposed by another subjective assessment, of the situation by the management, and nobody feels obliged to act upon the report. Moreover, the evaluation report will concentrate its analysis on the activities and outputs as the evaluators did not have the means and the information to discuss the higher level goals of the project.

2. Why does Project Reporting/Evaluation Concentrate on Processes rather than on Purposes?

Governments do realise that the purposes of projects and programmes are not the output or services provided, but the effect those outputs/services have on the target population. Thus the objectives of a rural drinking water project are seldom expressed in numbers of water points installed, but in terms of their supposed effect on health, productivity, quality of life, etc. The reluctance to measure the effects of social programmes is due to the nature of those programmes:

i) Disagreement on results

While everybody agrees that education has some positive effect on productivity, or that clean drinking water is related to the health status of the beneficiaries, there is considerable disagreement on how much these services contribute to the achievement of these goals. Because of this uncertainty on how much a service can be expected to contribute to these higher goals, politicians and project managers are reluctant to specify the effects of those services on the target population. Moreover since those effects are normally inflated to muster support for the projects, monitoring and evaluating of those effects can only be considered as a threat.

ii) Disagreement on measurements

Most social projects are supposed to affect the attitudes of the target population or their quality of life. Many managers believe that those aspects of the project cannot be measured and therefore not evaluated. As a matter of fact, the general terms used to express project goals and objectives prohibit an evaluation of those projects. However those general goals can be specified and at least partial measures to evaluate the effects of the project can be constructed.

iii) Disagreement about the ability of impact measurement

It has to be admitted that experience with impact evaluation has not proved the utility of those evaluations.[1] The failure is at least partly due to the following reasons:

1. See Selected References, Chapter IX.

- Evaluations are time consuming and skilled labour intensive.
The results of an evaluation are often not available when they are
needed by the management. To avoid high costs in labour and untimely
results, evaluations often use short cuts which are not compatible
with the relatively high technical rigour required to measure and
evaluate the often small changes a project brings about. Thus evaluation
results are often controversial or of only historical interest.

- Evaluations are not management oriented. Evaluations often
have their own dynamics. The questions they address are not the ones in
which the management is interested or management is perfectly aware
of the constraints and problems, but has no authority to act upon them.

iv)   Responsibilities of project management

Most of the time project management is responsible for the
delivery of services or for the production of an output, but not for the
effects the service or output is supposed to have on the beneficiaries.[1]
This is due to the fact that the project effects are not specified in the
project document, that there is disagreement on how much effect the
project document, that there is disagreement on how much effect the project can be reasonably assumed to have and how to measure these effects.
information only on inputs and outputs to show their efficiency in the
delivery of services. They will resent impact measurements of
promised effects which they know are inflated and for which they can
only get into trouble. To assure success of impact monitoring/
evaluation it is necessary that management is rewarded according to
their success in impact management and not purely on the account
of their effectiveness in delivering services.

3.   Evaluation Research

Governments are aware of the shortcomings of their monitoring/
evaluation activity as described above. For this reason most depart-
ments have selected one or two bigger projects where a special impact
evaluation effort is undertaken. Mostly evaluations are subcontracted
to a university or a research institute. Normally those evaluations
imply a considerable methodological effort, a large amount of data
gathering and a time consuming data analysis. This evaluation effort
is normally a separate entity attached to the project. The responsibility lies in the hand of academia and project management considers
the evaluation effort as an extraneous part to their project. Evaluation
in such a case responds more to the needs of the scientific interests
of the researcher/evaluator than to the needs of the project. The
consequences are the following:

---

1.   It is current practice that the head of projects are technicians (agronomists for rural
development, doctors for health projects and engineers for water supply, etc.). They have
been trained to provide a service in an efficient way.

- the evaluation becomes a research project with its own questions, requirements, funds and timetable. Therefore the requirements of the research project may conflict with the requirements of the project and conflict between the "evaluator" and project management is inevitable.

- the evaluation becomes a theory building exercise. The researcher is interested in the development of knowledge in the field concerned. His primary concern is therefore rigorous methodology and he considers changes in programmes, etc. proposed by the project management as an inadmissible interference into his test. On the other hand project management resents the interference of outsiders who tend to burden them with information requests and whom they consider as well paid parasites who have no responsibility for the success of the project.

- the evaluation provides information that is not digestable and not timely. The reports are written in a scientific language, they are bulky and attempt to show what happened and why it happened rather than providing recommendations on what should be done. Moreover those research efforts collect a large number of data which has to be processed and analysed. It is not infrequent that data processing and analysis take several years, in which case the results are mostly useless for the decision-makers.

Thus the evaluation efforts currently undertaken lead to the following results:

- either there is only performance monitoring of the project and no objective information is systematically gathered to monitor and evaluate the impact of the project;

- or a special effort is made to evaluate the impact of the project and the evaluation becomes a costly and time-consuming research project, which is not related to the management of the project.

Both results are unsatisfactory for management purposes.

III

THE MAJOR PROBLEMS OF CURRENT MONITORING/EVALUATION EFFORTS

1. Definition of monitoring/evaluation

Monitoring/evaluation in its general sense[1] is used here to describe a systematic framework to collect and analyse information on events associated with the implementation of a policy, programme or project with a view to improving their management. From this definition some characteristics can be derived:
- Monitoring/evaluation relates to management. If there is no management of a social programme, there can be no relevant monitoring/evaluation system;
- Management implies a certain amount of planning. A management system has to know what it wants and what information it will need. Only if information needs are foreseen can they be collected in a systematic way and be available when they are needed.

2. The utility of a monitoring/evaluation system

The purpose of monitoring/evaluation is to improve management of social services by:
- providing timely information on the success/failure of policy, programmes and projects;
- assuring that the information is used by the decision-makers.

To ensure that the information provided by monitoring/evaluation is useful to the decision-maker it is necessary that there is agreement on the information that is needed for the management of the project. This is only possible if the following conditions are fulfilled:
- the impact of the project is defined in measurable terms;
- there is agreement that the information collected truly reflects the degree of attainment of the project's objectives;
- there is a clear understanding of how the project's inputs and outputs are related to the project purpose, i.e. there is a logic to the project that permits identification of testable hypotheses;

---

1. For the definition of various activities falling within the term "monitoring/evaluation", see next Chapter.

- project management knows for what type of decisions the information will be used and what the relative importance of that information in the decision-making process is. This information is crucial for determining the cost-effectiveness of various designs to collect the information.

3. The major problems of current monitoring/evaluation efforts

The basic problem in project monitoring/evaluation is the absence of management by objectives. "Evaluation cannot prescribe management actions. Rather, the needs of management should define evaluations".[1] If a project or programme is characterised by "vague goals, strong promises and weak effects"[2] there is little monitoring and evaluation can contribute to. The absence of a clear management line has the following consequences:

- lack of agreement on expected results, means to measure those results and the relationship between inputs, outputs and higher goals. It is not up to the evaluator to design the project in technical terms. His attempt to define a vague programme in measurable and logical terms will necessarily fail, as he will thus test his framework and not the management's one. Under those conditions management is sure to reject the monitoring/evaluation results as irrelevant and "theoretical";

- lack of dialogue between project management and evaluators. The role of the evaluator is to make explicit the logic of the project so that it can be evaluated. To ensure that the results of the evaluation are used it is necessary that the evaluation framework expresses the way project management sees the project's logic. It is thus necessary that there is a close dialogue between project management and evaluators right from the start of the project. This is mostly not the case. Project evaluation is tagged onto a project somewhere during its life and project management and evaluators function in isolation side by side;

- lack of agreement on what monitoring/evaluation can do and on who is the user of the results. Project management is often asking the impossible of evaluation. Certain questions can simply not be answered by monitoring/evaluation, especially if one considers all the constraints put upon the evaluation. To avoid a disenchantment by project managers and evaluators alike it is necessary to clearly determine what monitoring/evaluation can do and under what conditions.

1. Pamela Horst, Joe N. Nay et al., "Programme Management and the Federal Evaluator" in Public Administration Review, July/August 1974, p. 306.

2. Ilene Nagel Bernstein, Evaluation Research: Development and Dissemination of Evaluation Techniques, UNESCO Symposium on "Evaluation Methodology for Social Action Programmes and Projects", Washington D.C., September 20-24, 1976.

Moreover, the users of project evaluation have to be identified. The information needs of project, programme and policy managers are rather different. If there is confusion about the different uses of the monitoring/evaluation results there is a great chance that the results will be rejected by all three levels of management.

IV

TYPES OF EVALUATION

The term of evaluation is used for everything from a cursory project visit to a very elaborate evaluation research project. All activities that provide information for the management of projects or programmes are summed up in the terms of monitoring/evaluation. Much disagreement on monitoring/evaluation techniques is due to the fact that people speak about different types of evaluation. It is therefore necessary to define those types of evaluation. [1]

The two criteria used to define the different types of evaluation are:
- evaluation as a management tool. This criterion is necessary to deliminate evaluation ranging from research to administrative devices to control project execution;
- the purpose of evaluation. The use one intends to make of evaluation results determines the type of data to be collected, the degree of reliability and therefore the design of the evaluation and the significance and conclusiveness of the information collected. A typology based on the purpose of the evaluation is therefore necessary when we attempt to discuss the "worth" of various types of evaluation.

1. Accounting and auditing are the traditional means of ensuring that funds are spent in the way they have been authorised and comply with administrative regulations. They are administrative, not management tools and therefore cannot be considered as types of monitoring/evaluation, as defined here.

2. Project reporting system. The traditional reporting systems limit themselves to the financial and physical implementation of the project. Most of the time they are administrative control devices and therefore cannot be considered as part of a monitoring/evaluation system.

However, in a modern management system the project reporting goes further than that and becomes an integral part of the monitoring exercise.

---

1. Each type of evaluation has its own purpose and requirements. The task of setting up an evaluation system is to choose among the different evaluation types those which are adapted to the information needs and the capacity of the project management.

3.   Monitoring.   Monitoring is "the collection and management use of specific information on events associated with the operation of a project or group of projects".[1]   The monitoring exercise is supposed to provide the necessary information to assess progress towards the achievement of project objectives.   Thus project monitoring needs to provide information not only on the project itself, but also on the environment and on its effects on the target group.   The design of a monitoring system consists basically in the development of a data collection and reporting system that provides the necessary information to assess progress in project or programme goal achievement.   Monitoring is a continuous task during the whole life of the project.   It therefore relies heavily on project or programme management for the collection and presentation of the information.

The data to be collected depend on how well the project has been analysed and on the resources available.   The information collected should be selective and management oriented.   The minimum information necessary to assess the progress of a project/programme is:
  - some information on what the project/programme is doing;
  - some measurements of the effects of the project;
  - some measurements to identify the target group;
  - some criteria to assess the effects.
The results of monitoring are used:
  - by the project/programme management to know where the project stands;
  - by the funding agency as an information tool to assess project performance in substantive terms.

4.   Process evaluation.   Monitoring is supposed to provide information on what is happening, process evaluation (also called formative, developmental or on-going evaluation) on why it is happening (or why it is not happening).   It is an internal management tool designed to serve the operational needs of project or programme personnel. While monitoring is a continuous exercise, process evaluation is an ad hoc attempt to solve a specific problem.   Process evaluation is particularly useful in experimental projects, where little is known about how to produce the desired effects.   "Process evaluation can be used with considerable effectiveness to improve the performance of flexible treatments such as television programmes which can be technically modified rather simply and at relatively minor costs prior to the dissemination".[2]

---

1.   John D. Waller et al., Monitoring for Government Agencies, p. 5, The Urban Institute, February 1976, Washington D.C.

2.   Peter H. Rossi, Sonia R. Wright, "Evaluation Research: An Assessment of Current Theory, Practice and Politics", p. 29, Paper submitted to a UNESCO conference on Evaluation Research, October 1976.

Process evaluation is normally tied to the results of the monitoring exercise: before explaining why something happens it is necessary to know what happened. Howerer this is not necessarily so. A monitoring system might not be feasible for a given project: rather than attempt to have an overview of what is happening, project management might prefer to collect information on a few cases in which the project seems to have been successful and compare those cases with situations where the project seems to have failed. Such a comparison might provide very useful information on the reasons of failure and success and thus lead to a significant improvement of project management. There exists no abstract rule on which of these two types of information gathering is more appropriate. This will depend on the specific project situation and on the resources available. The choice does not depend on the intellectual "neatness" of the approach, but on the usefulness of the information gathered. The only criterion to choose among different types of evaluation is the potential of the evaluation to improve project management and whether the information collected is the most relevant that can be obtained given the constraints under which the project is working.

5. Implementation evaluation is basically a control device. It is used by the programme or policy manager to determine whether the individual projects have been executed according to the guidelines. The programme that policy or programme managers have in mind might be quite different from the programme that is actually executed in the field. Programmes often get transformed by the people who execute them. It is therefore important to find out "... what actually transpires at the point of delivery".[1]

6. Impact evaluation or ex-post evaluation attempts to identify all the effects of a project whether anticipated or not. It not only measures the effects of the project, but also attempts to validate or invalidate the logic of the project, i.e. the hypotheses that are linking the project input to output, output to purpose and purpose to objective. Thus impact evaluation has four goals:[2]
- identify whether stated goals have been achieved;
- attribute the identified effects to the programme, i.e. rule out rival hypotheses; while impact evaluation might do that by circumstantial evidence, evaluation research will use statistical methods to rule out rival hypotheses;
- determine conditions under which project is most effective;
- delineate any unanticipated consequences or side effects of the implementation programme.

1. Peter H. Rossi, Sonia R. Wright, op. cit., p. 31.
2. Howard E. Freeman, "The Present Status of Evaluation Research", p. 42, unpublished paper submitted to a UNESCO Conference on Evaluation Research, Paris, August 1976.

Impact evaluation distinguishes itself from process evaluation and monitoring in the following respects:
- impact evaluation is done at the end of the project or some time after the end of the project; this does not mean that impact evaluation is planned and executed at the end of the project. Impact evaluation requires information on the situation at the beginning of the project and during its execution. The decision whether to undertake an impact evaluation or not has therefore to be taken at the beginning of the project;
- impact evaluation is comprehensive: it addresses the question what has happened and why it has happened. Since impact evaluation attempts to attribute the effects to the programme, it necessarily includes an implementation evaluation. It is obviously important to know what sort of programme has (or has not) produced the measured effects. An impact evaluation without an implementation evaluation risks attributing effects to a treatment that never existed or attributing the failure of a programme to the content of the programme rather than to its faulty execution;[1]
- impact evaluation provides information for programme and policy managers, not project management.

7.   Evaluation research is "any scientifically based activity designed to assess the operation and impact of public policy".[2] Evaluation research and impact evaluation address the same questions, however they may differ considerably in terms of methodology and thus in the degree of confidence one can put into the results of the evaluation.[3] While any assessment of the impact of a project might be called impact evaluation, evaluation research uses by definition social science research methods to measure the impact of policy questions. Evaluation research is useful to policy management and is particularly adapted to policy questions that have been well structured. Evaluation research, though a more powerful tool than the other evaluations, is not necessarily the best one. It would seem that a rational policy making exercise would attempt to analyse and structure the functioning of a policy intervention through the collection of circumstantial evidence (formative, impact evaluation). Only once the process is well analysed and once it is possible to formulate clear hypotheses, evaluation research would be used to arrive at a definitive conclusion concerning the value of a given policy action.

The different type of evaluation and their characteristics are summarised in Figure XIII.

---

1.   Rossi/Wright, Ibid., p. 55/56.

2.   Peter H. Rossi, Sonia R. Wright, op. cit., p. 1.

3.   Example: Evaluation research requires that inputs be kept constant during the execution of the project.

Figure XII. TYPES OF EVALUATION AND THEIR CHARACTERISTICS

TYPE OF EVALUATION / CHARACTERISTICS	FUNCTION	PURPOSE	PRIMARY USER	TIMING	TYPE OF INFORMATION	WHO COLLECTS INFORMATION	EXPECTED RESULTS
Accounting and auditing	Administrative	Control	Central administration	Accounting: continuous; Auditing: periodical	Financial	Project agents	Improved financial administration
Reporting (Traditional)	Administrative	Control	Central administration	Periodical	Input/output	Project management	Improved administration of products and services
Reporting/monitoring	Management	Determine what is happening	Project management	Continuous	Input/output purpose, intervening variables	Project management	Improved management of projects
Process evaluation	Management	Determine why it is happening	Project management	Ad hoc or periodical	Input/output process, purpose	Project management; outside help	More efficient management of project components
Implementation evaluation	Management and administration	Determine execution of project components	Project management	Periodical	Input, process	Programme management	Improved management of content of project activities
Impact or ex post evaluation	Management	Determine effects of project	Policy management	Data collection beginning/end of project; Analysis: end of project	Input/output purpose, goal, hypotheses	Outside institution in collaboration with policy management	Improved programme management
Evaluation research	Management	Determine effects of policy	Policy management and planning	Data collection periodical; Analysis: end of project	Input/output purpose, goal, hypotheses	Research institutions universities	Improved policy management and planning

V

SETTING UP A MONITORING/EVALUATION SYSTEM FOR A GOVERNMENT AGENCY

Evaluation is considered as one management tool among others for government agencies to improve public policy.   Thus the worth of evaluation depends on:
- the use of the evaluation results in the decision-making process and in management;
- the extent to which the evaluation results improve social policy or the delivery of social services.

Whether evaluation results are used in management and decision-making depends on the management structure and the way decisions are made in an agency.   Each structure needs or uses different information and thus a different evaluation system.   Since management structures define evaluation needs, the evaluation system has to be adapted to that structure.   Therefore, no two evaluation systems will be the same.

The setting up of a monitoring/evaluation system for a Government Agency requires the following analyses.

1.   Determination of the Information Needs of a Government Agency

Not all Government Agencies need or can use an information system.   To determine what sort of information a Government needs and how to collect it, it is necessary to:

a)   Analyse the management structure of the agency

If a Government Agency is only administering a programme and not managing it, there is little a monitoring/evaluation system can contribute.   In such a situation the task of the evaluator would be to clearly indicate that the management structure has to be reviewed before an evaluation system can be introduced.   Thus, before proposing a specific monitoring/evaluation system it is necessary for the evaluator to review the management structure and to interview the agency staff so as to determine:
- what is being managed by the agency;
- how is it being managed;
- who is managing; and
- who wants a monitoring/evaluation system.

b)   Determine what information should be available to the agency

Once the decision-making and management structure is understood it is possible to determine what sort of information should be
available and could be used within the management structure.   The
evaluator can only suggest types of information: it is up to the decision-
maker and manager to say whether they would use the information were
it available and what importance that information would have for their
decisions.

c)   Determine what information can be collected

Management has a tendency to inflate its information needs when
its decisions are discussed in abstract.   A confrontation with what the
information gathering exercise would imply in terms of skills, funds
and time will permit the cutting down of those needs to the bare
minimum.   The evaluator should clearly indicate if any information,
though important for management, cannot be collected within the
constraints imposed on a monitoring/evaluation exercise.   There are
many reasons why a monitoring/evaluation system might not be able to
collect certain informations:
- the concepts implied in the information required are too vague
  to be expressed in quantitative terms;
- the information required would necessitate manpower and funds
  exceeding the benefit of the information;
- the information could be collected but not within the time frame
  in which it is needed.
The timeliness of information, i.e. its availability when management needs it, is a very important constraint, not only for what sort
of information can be collected, but also for the methodology and hence
the accuracy of the information collected.   As a principle it can be
said that information that is available after an irreversible decision
has been taken is useless whatever the level of confidence we can put
into that information.[1]   Whether information with a low level of
confidence is better than no information depends on the costs and the
type of decision for which the information is used.

2.   Determination of Who Needs the Information

The user of the information generated by a monitoring/evaluation
system will determine:
- What has to be monitored or evaluated.   It is necessary that
the evaluation system reflects the manager's understanding of the

---

1.   This does not exclude the possibility that the information might be very useful for some
other users than the specific management considered in the example.

programme or project.[1] In more complicated administrative set ups a
programme might be perceived in different ways by different levels.
If the monitoring/evaluation system does not use the same perception
of the programme as the intended user of its results, the user will
discard the conclusions as irrelevant or theoretical. It is thus
necessary that the monitoring/evaluation system is based on the
intended user's perception of the programme and not on a social scientist's or a "political" view of the programme, unless the social scientist or the politician are the users of the evaluation results.
   -   The type of information to be collected. The type of information
to be collected will vary according to the management level. It is clear
that a project manager will need different information from a policy-
maker. It is, therefore, important to clearly indicate which type of
information is addressed to which level of management by distinguishing:
   - project management;
   - programme management;
   - policy management.
   -   The timeliness of information. It is necessary to know the user
of the information in order to determine when the information is needed.
Project management is interested in quick and continuous feedback.
Policy makers need the information at specific points of time.
   -   The presentation of information will depend on its user.
Information for policy makers will be aggregated and short, project
managers will need much more disaggregated information.

3.   Determination of the Degree of Confidence Needed

   The degree of confidence needed depends on:
   - for what the information will be used;
   - what degree of confidence can be achieved within the given
     constraints.
   The degree of confidence we can have in given information depends
on how the information has been collected, i. e. on the design of the
monitoring/evaluation system. Unfortunately, higher degrees of
confidence are mostly associated with more complicated designs, i. e.
with more costs. The trade-offs between costs and confidence level
depend on the use made of the information. If the information is a
decisive factor for a decision, and if the decision is a very important
one, the decision-maker will want to have a high degree of confidence
and is thus ready to pay a higher price for that information. If the

---

1.   This does not mean that the management's perception of the project will be used, even
if it is manifestly wrong. The evaluation framework will be the outcome of a dialogue between management and evaluator and the final design should reflect a common view. If no
common view can be achieved, and management's perception of the project is clearly wrong,
the project is "unevaluable" from a management point of view.

information is not very important a factor for the decision, or if the decision has only minor consequences, the decision-maker will not be ready to pay a high price for a higher level of confidence. The level of confidence will also depend on the accuracy required to make the decision, e. g. whether a literacy programme has a success rate of 65 or 75% might have little influence on the decision for which this information is used; on the other hand a 0. 1% chance of fatal side effects might be enough to ban a new medication.

Thus, what is important is not an abstract level of confidence, but that there is an agreement on the specific level of confidence and accuracy needed for a given use of the information collected.

4.   The choice of an evaluation system

The above analysis will provide the necessary information for choosing a monitoring/evaluation system which:
- provides the necessary information for the given management structure;
- takes into account the resources (time, skills, funds) available;
- is cost-effective.

An agency, with a given amount of resources for monitoring/ evaluation, will not monitor/evaluate all the programmes and projects:
- some programmes might go on, whatever their results, e. g. the government might finance a particular programme to placate a pressure group. Monitoring/evaluation would have no influence on the decision concerning the programme; [1]
- some programmes/projects might not be worth evaluating, e. g. , policy makers do not agree on what the programme is supposed to bring about. If there is no agreement on expected results of a programme, the monitoring/evaluation system cannot show whether these results have been achieved.

Moreover, an agency will not use the same type of monitoring/ evaluation for each programme. For some programmes the management might want only some circumstantial evidence that the programme is doing what it is supposed to, for others they might need more scientific evidence. For an exploratory programme, the management might be interested in different approaches rather than in the overall success and thus opt for some ad hoc process evaluations rather than

---

1.   It is not pretended that the evaluation of such a programme would be of no use to anybody: to a politician or a research institute the evaluation of those projects might be of high interest. However, a Government Agency using an evaluation system to improve its management of a social programme should allocate its scarce evaluation resources to the monitoring and evaluation of programmes that can be changed, i.e. where the potential benefits in terms of better management are the highest for a given amount of evaluation resources.

an ongoing monitoring system. However, for some social measures, management might want to have a once and for all answer concerning its effects and cost-effectiveness and thus decide on an all out effort in the form of evaluation research.

Thus this analysis should provide:
- a list of programmes and projects which should be monitored/ evaluated;
- the type of monitoring/evaluation required for the specific programmes/projects.

The specific steps and results of this analysis are outlined in Figure XIII.

Figure XIII. SETTING UP A MONITORING/EVALUATION SYSTEM FOR A GOVERNMENT AGENCY

Analytical steps   ### Products

1. **Analysis of management structure**

    Decision-making procedure → Diagram

    Information needs → Preliminary theoretical list of information requirements

    Capacity of information collection → Feasible list of information requirements

2. **Scrutiny of information users**

    Willingness to use information → Feasible list of useful information requirements

    Timing of information needs → Feasible list of useful information that can be made available when needed

    Acceptability of the presentation of information → Reporting system for the information

3. **Scrutiny of the uses of information**

    - Importance of information for decision

    - Importance of decision for programme   Required accuracy of information

    - Information gathering capabilities → Feasible accuracy of information

4. **Choice of an evaluation programme**

    - Comparison: needs and resources   List of programmes and projects to be monitored/evaluated

    - Comparison of different types of evaluations   Type of monitoring/evaluation design appropriate for specific information needs

136

VI

SETTING UP A MONITORING/EVALUATION SYSTEM
FOR A SPECIFIC PROGRAMME OR PROJECT

Once it has been decided that a specific programme or project should be monitored or evaluated, the following information will determine the type of evaluation system chosen:[1]

- What should be measured: it is necessary to base the evaluation design on the project design, so that there is agreement among the various actors about what are the crucial issues in the project that should be measured.

- For whom should it be measured: the identification of the users of the results of an evaluation is crucial to ensure that the evaluation corresponds to the user's perceptions and thus will be used.

- For what should it be measured: it is necessary to know the use that will be made of the information collected to determine the necessary sensitivity of the measures and the degree of accuracy needed.

- How should it be measured: it is necessary that there is a consensus between project management and monitors/evaluators whether a proposed measure really indicates a change in the desired direction.

- How the data should be collected: it is necessary to determine the design of the evaluation system which provides the desired level of confidence and that everybody agrees that the achieved accuracy in information will be adequate for the proposed user of the information.

- When and in which form the information is needed: information collection can involve considerable time. To ensure that the information is available when needed it is necessary to foresee the information need in advance. Moreover, information to be useful has to be physically and mentally accessible. A short résumé providing the specific information needed by a policy-maker has a high chance of being used. A long report is inaccessible to a busy policy-maker.

---

1. The analytical steps are the same as in the preceding Chapter. The analysis, however takes place at a different level of abstraction. The different steps are therefore discussed in greater detail.

- Who collects, analyses and presents the information: this information is necessary to adapt the monitoring/evaluation system to the management realities of a programme/project. The time needed to analyse and present the information should not be underestimated.

1. What Should be Monitored/Evaluated

To determine what should be monitored/evaluated the following information has to be collected:

i) Goal specification

a) The problem: to know what we want to monitor/evaluate we have to know what effects the programme/project is supposed to have. As discussed earlier, programme goals are often vague and inflated. Thus, different people associated with the same project might have d different perceptions of what the project is supposed to and can achieve.

b) Establish agreement about project goals: the evaluator cannot define the goals of a project: this has to be done by the decision-maker. However, the evaluator has to assure that the users of his evaluation results agree that the goals he measures are the relevant ones. The evaluator will play the role of a catalyser between different levels of policy making and ensure that the proposed goals to be monitored are agreed upon by the users of his evaluation results. The various goals held by different managers may not be reconcilable: the political goals by the sponsor of the programme might not coincide with the ones of project management. The evaluator will attempt to monitor the project the way it is seen and understood by the user of his monitoring/evaluation results and not the project that should or could exist.

c) Express the project goals in measurable terms: project goals often seem to be clearly identified. However, "... what at first seems clear often evaporates when the test of measurability is applied".[1] Sometimes project goals are expressed in such vague terms that it is impossible to express them in measurable terms. The evaluator again attempts to clarify the intents of the decision-maker.[2] However, he cannot do the goal specification by himself: if no agreement can be reached on who the various goals can be expressed in measurable terms, this means that the decision-makers do not really know what they want the project to achieve and the evaluator should clearly indicate that such a programme or project cannot be usefully monitored or evaluated.

---

1. Horst, Pamela et al., op. cit., p. 302.

2. The procedure to express goals in measurable terms is the operationalisation of goals discussed in Part II of the paper. The project is not evaluable if no agreement can be reached about the hierarchy of goals and their inter-relationships.

d)   Define the yardstick: once the goals are set in measurable terms it is necessary to determine "how much progress toward the goal marks success".[1]   Monitoring/evaluation consist mainly of one type of analysis: "a comparison of what was planned with what is being achieved".[2]   For monitoring/evaluation purposes it is necessary to define before the project's effects are measured:
- what level of measurement can be considered as a success;
- what deviation from that level would make a difference to the manager.

A clear identification of the effects of the monitoring evaluation results on management makes it possible to ensure that project management is specific about its information requirements and agrees in advance on the accuracy and confidence level which are required to influence its management decisions.

e)   The problem of unanticipated effects: the effects of a project are normally expressed in terms of the expected objectives the project is supposed to achieve.   But most projects have also unexpected effects.   Unexpected effects escape the monitoring/evaluation design: since they are not expected it is impossible to include their measurement into the monitoring design.   There are two ways of diminishing the unexpected effects:
- through better analysis of the project rationale, thus permitting identification of as many effects as possible, whether positive or negative;
- by explicitly querying the relationship of the project to all major development problems and not only to those, the solution of which is the purpose of the project.[3]

It has to be admitted that no evaluation framework can ensure that all unexpected effects are captured.   The dynamic setting of an action programme even complicates the issue: the problematic, the environment, the programme may be altered during the execution and the monitoring/evaluation system identified at the beginning might become irrelevant.   Thus it is necessary to examine during project execution whether the goals and measurements identified at the beginning of the project continue to be relevant.

ii)   The specification of the programme

a)   The problem: most social programmes do specify what activities should be undertaken.   However, they do not indicate how these activities should be executed and how each activity relates to the

---

1.   Carol H. Weiss, Evaluation Research, p. 32, Prentice Hall, 1972.
2.   John D. Waller et al. Monitoring for Government Agencies, p. 48, The Urban Institute, 1976.
3.   For a more detailed analysis of multiple goal setting for projects see Part II.

total programme. Thus, under the same programme name there might exist many projects with rather different activities and outcomes. There are two elements of project design which have to be specified and agreed upon to ensure the evaluability of a programme:
- the programme elements;
- the logic of the programme.

b) Specification of programme elements: there are three reasons why it is difficult to have explicit programme elements defined at the start of a project:
- decision-makers do not conceive their efforts in segmented parts: "In the minds of some, doing so may have undesirable consequences, for programme elements, when viewed independently are more open to criticism than if a total defense package is described"; [1]
- the decision-makers often have enough of an understanding of a social problem to propose the actions that should be taken, but not enough knowledge of the local situation to propose how the interventions should be handled;
- many inputs of a programme are "so called professional know-how ... Particularly professionals with status and prestige are offended and affronted by the idea that they must expose what they do".[2]
Thus there is inevitably conflict between the evaluator's needs of specificity and the professional's perception of the individuality of each action in its setting.

An explicit agreement on elements of a project and on their content is essential to ensure that the monitoring/evaluation results correspond to the needs of the management.

c) Specification of the programme's logic: evaluation in its wide sense, attempts to show what has happened and why it has happened. Evaluation should provide the information necessary to validate, invalidate or modify the hypotheses on which the project was based. If there exists no explicit framework for the project it will be impossible to monitor or evaluate the project. "Tests cannot be designed for people who are unable to, or refuse to state their assumptions".[3] It is important that the project logic on which the monitoring and evaluation design is based reflects the way project or programme management understands the project and not on the evaluator's view of the functioning of the project.

iii) The results of the specification exercise

Social programmes are often very complex: they involve people, styles and procedures; their implementation varies from place to

1. Howard Freeman, op. cit., p. 26.
2. Ibid, p. 26.
3. Horst, Pamela, et al., op. cit., p. 304.

place, from person to person. The specification of the programme
is necessary to determine to what the outcomes are to be attributed and
to determine what worked and what did not work. The programme can
be described by the following variables:

    -   input variables: the measurement of a few crucial variables
will focus of attention on the important dimensions of the programme;

    -   process variables: they permit the description of how project
inputs are supposed to lead to the expected outcomes;

    -   output variables: focus attention on expected outcomes at
different levels which are needed to attain the project's or programme's
objectives. The different outcomes are structured in a goal matrix that
provides the logical structure to link various outputs to project purpose
and objectives;

    -   assumption indicators: the link of events within a goal matrix
are based on a number of assumptions, e.g. professional training is
linked to the objective of increased income by the assumptions that jobs
are available and that salaries take into account professional skills.
The project has no control over those assumptions. Nevertheless they
have to be verified as the project's outcome will depend on them.

2.   What Can Be Monitored/Evaluated?

    The preceding paragraphs have indicated what should be measured
in a monitoring/evaluation system. However, within each category
mentioned, there are many variables that are interesting to study. Most
projects have limited resources for monitoring/evaluation and very
often the resources are so limited that a discussion of what could be
measured becomes irrelevant. Thus it is necessary to make a choice
among the variables and to determine:

    -   what is the bare minimum of information necessary to make a
monitoring/evaluation system worthwhile;

    -   what is the best use of the monitoring/evaluation resources
available.

    As mentioned earlier the "worth" of an information depends on its
use. Thus, to choose the variables to be monitored/evaluated it will
be necessary to know:

    -   the importance of the variable for the success of the project:
the more critical the variable for the success of the project, the more
important it is for the management to know how the variables develops;

    -   the importance of a change in the variable to management actions.
Some variables may be critical to the success of the project, however
management has no alternative actions open to it if the expected and
real value of the variable differ. Such a variable would have a lower
priority than another critical variable that can be influenced by management decisions;

- the degree of uncertainty of the information: if management has reasons to believe that there is little chance that the expected value will differ from the real value, the monitoring of the variable becomes less important,[1] e. g. if we know from past experiences that graduates from a training programme have no problems to find employment and the job market study indicates that their skills will be in short supply for the time of the project, the monitoring of employment after the study programme becomes much less important than when we have very little information on the availability of jobs for the skills taught in the training programme;

- the cost of collecting the information: some information can be collected at very low cost; for other information it is necessary to set up complicated designs and data collection procedures. Thus information that is useful, yet not crucial might be collected because its costs are very low. Some crucial information might not be collected because its costs are prohibitive or because the information cannot be collected within the time frame required. However, the decision is again not as clear cut: the costs of collecting information is not fixed, but depends on the accuracy and confidence level we try to achieve.

There are two techniques that can be used to identify the crucial information needs and to determine the benefit (or cost) of more (or less) information:

a) The project performance network chart.[2] The project performance network chart is used to identify the critical variables of a project and to show their interrelationships. It permits the identification of crucial problems in project execution and their importance for the success of the project. It attempts to show graphically the interrelationships between time, the input, process, and output variables, and the assumption indicators (see above). It attempts to show what happens to the project if one of the actual measurements differs from the planned results. By identifying the relative importance of the variables to project success, the network chart provides a basis for the monitoring/evaluation effort.

---

1. This does not mean that any outcome that is considered to be "sure" should not be measured. Experience has shown that factors that were taken for "granted" did not occur. However if we have to make a choice between monitoring a variable that we consider as certain and another one that is highly uncertain, we will have to abandon the monitoring of the former one. The decision is however not a black and white one: it might be possible to use some low cost cursory measure for the "sure" variable to maintain some circumstantial evidence that the outcome is in fact occurring.

2. The Project Performance Tracking System (PPT) is used in USAID projects. This section follows the AID instructions on that subject. See USAID Handbook 3 Project Assistance, Part I, Chapter 3, Appendix G, p. 1-10.

The basic steps in drawing up a network chart are:[1]

- select the most critical indicators of performance for the project: the analysis of the elements, the logic and the purpose of the project undertaken earlier will permit the identification of the elements that should be included into the network. Only the most crucial ones for project success will be included;

- estimate the date at which each indicator is critical to the success of the project: the "critical" date is not the "expected" date but the latest date at which the project management could intervene to ensure that the delay has no irreversible consequences on the planned purpose and objectives of the project;

- show how they relate to each other on a chart in a kind of "road map" for tracking performance:[2] all the critical performance indicators are brought together and related to each other and time. The purpose is to visualise the functioning of the project. One has succeeded if the chart and indicators permit its reader to grasp the functioning of the project and to identify the crucial issues in its implementation. A USAID Handbook example of the chart is reproduced in Figure XIV;

- review and discuss the chart with all people who have an interest in the project: this will allow clarification of the chart and assurance that the logic expressed in it is shared by project management.

Thus the project performance network chart helps the project analyst to identify the most important elements of a project that should be monitored or evaluated.

b)   The use of subjective probabilities. The project performance network chart permits identification of the importance of the various project elements to the success of the project. It provides however, no information about the degree of uncertainty of the various indicators. Baysian procedures[3] permit determination of the importance of uncertainty to the decision-making process and subjective probabilities permit the introduction of uncertainty and risks into the project analysis. Baysian procedures permit "... in fact encourage, quantitative combination of evidence from different courses, different lines of enquiry and different techniques of investigation ... In particular, they make it easy to combine, in a formally appropriate numerical way, judgements with experimental or other empirical data".[4]   The decision-

---

1.   USAID Handbook 3, "Project Assistance", op. cit., p. 2-5.

2.   The Project Performance Network Chart is conceptually related to Programme Evaluation Review Technique/Critical Path Method (PERT/CPM). However, since the elements included in the chart are limited to the most critical ones, the chart is much less complicated and can be drawn and understood by non-technicians.

3.   For details, see Selected Annotated References, Part II.

4.   Ward Edwards, Marcia Guttentag, Kurt Snapper, "A decision theoretic approach to evaluation research" in Handbook of Evaluation Research, Vol. I, p. 151, Elmer L. Struening Eds.

Figure XIV

A PROJECT PERFORMANCE NETWORK CHART

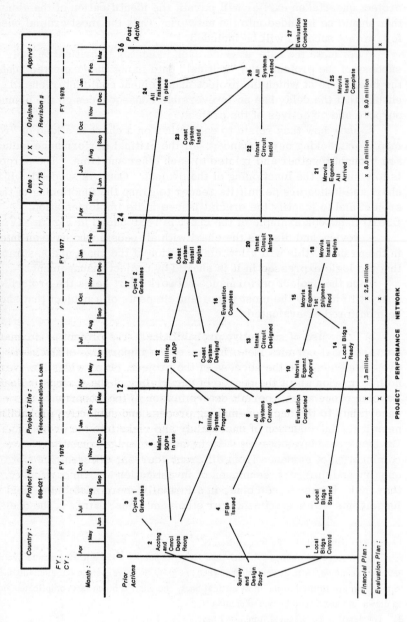

144

COUNTRY	PROJECT No.	PROJECT TITLE:	DATE:	ORIGINAL	Apprvd:
	669-021	TELECOMMUNICATIONS LOAN	4/1/75	X REVISION	

CPI	DESCRIPTION	
1.	4/15/75	Contract signed for construction of warehouse and Paynesville Exchange Bldg.
2.	5/15/75	Reorganisation of Accounting and Commercial departments completed
3.	7/30/75	First cycle of in-country training completed
4.	7/30/75	Invitation-for-Bids issued on 3 systems
5.	8/15/75	Warehouse and Exchange buildings started
6.	12/30/75	Standard Operating Procedures for maintenance and spare parts operations in use
7.	1/30/76	Programming and auxiliary procedures for computerized billing completed
8.	2/15/76	Contracts signed for three systems
9.	2/15/76	Evaluation completed
10.	4/30/76	Design and specifications for Greater Monrovia System approved
11.	6/15/76	Design of the Coast System approved
12.	6/30/76	Computerized billing operating successfully
13.	7/15/76	International circuit system design approved
14.	7/31/76	Warehouse and Exchange buildings ready for occupancy
15.	10/15/76	First shipment of equipment for Greater Monrovia System
16.	10/30/76	Evaluation completed
17.	11/15/76	Second cycle of in-country training complete trainees now on job
18.	1/15/77	Installation of Greater Monrovia equipment begins
19.	1/15/77	Coastal System installation begins
20.	2/28/77	All equipment for the International Circuit manufactured and tested at plant
21.	7/30/77	All equipment for Greater Monrovia System arrived
22.	9/30/77	All equipment for International Circuit installed
23.	9/30/77	All equipment for Coastal System installed
24.	1/30/78	At least trainees now on jobs in the system
25.	2/15/78	Greater Monrovia installation of equipment complete
26.	3/31/78	All systems tested and certified
27.	5/15/78	Evaluation completed

maker's probability distribution of the planned event will provide the necessary information to judge the importance of monitoring a critical performance indicator. The amount of time and money the manager is ready to spend to monitor a critical performance indicator is obviously much higher if he considers that the chance the planned outcome occurs is 50 percent than when he considers the probability of achieving the planned results to be 99 percent.

Thus the calculation of subjective probabilities for each critical performance indicator will allow inclusion of uncertainty into the determination of what should or should not be monitored.

c) The results of the analysis:[1] The analyses so far have provided us with the crucial information to decide what type of monitoring/evaluation system is adapted to a given situation and what sort of evaluation design can be envisaged by identifying:
- who uses the results of project monitoring/evaluation;
- when and for what are the results needed;
- what should and can be monitored.
This information is needed to determine:
- the type of monitoring/evaluation system;
- the design of the evaluation exercise.
We have discussed the different types of monitoring/evaluation systems earlier. The identification of the information needs and uses will permit the choosing of the type of monitoring/evaluation that is the most adapted to the specific management needs of the project/programme.

We still need, however, to determine how to collect the information needed.

3. The Choice of a Monitoring/Evaluation Design

Introduction

A monitoring/evaluation system is supposed to provide accurate information on:
- the magnitude of changes that can be observed;
- which of those changes can be attributed to the project activities.
The design of a monitoring/evaluation study is "an organisation of measures in ways to permit demonstration of achievement or non-achievement of the intended effects of the programme".[2]

The choice of the evaluation design will determine how much confidence can be placed in the results of the evaluation. There are many different threats to the validity of evaluation results:

---

1. For a summary of the analytical steps and their results, see Figure XV.
2. Office of Nutrition, TAB, USAID, A Field Guide for Evaluation of Nutrition Evaluation, June 1975, p. 19.

Figure XV. SETTING UP A MONITORING/EVALUATION
SYSTEM FOR A SPECIFIC PROGRAMME OR PROJECT

Analytical steps   Products

1. Specification of programme

    - goal specification   ———► goal matrix

    - definition of yardsticks ———► objectively verifiable
                                        indicators

    - specification of pro-   ———► determination of process and
      gramme elements   input variables

    - specification of pro-   ———► determination of hypotheses
      gramme logical

┌──┐
│   The evaluable model of the project   │
└──┘

2. Critical analysis of the
    project's logic

    - project performance   ———► list of critical variables
      network

    - risk and uncertainty   ———► list of high-risk variables
      analysis

┌──┐
│   The feasible model for project monitoring/evaluation │
└──┘

3. Critical analysis of the
    evaluation framework

    - discussion of evaluation ———► accepted evaluation frame-
      design with project man-   work
      agement

    - analysis of use of   ———► type of evaluations required
      information

    - analysis of costs and ———► cost-effective evaluation
      benefits of evaluation   framework
      design

┌──┐
│   The practical model for project monitoring/evaluation │
└──┘

- Internal validity: is "the ability of a research design to yield unbiased estimates of the effects of the treatment administered".[1] The evaluation design should allow the ruling out of competing explanations for the effects of the project.
- External validity: monitoring/evaluation systems collect information on a few "representative" individuals to make inferences about the effects of the programme on all the individuals to whom the policy is being applied. It must be possible to generalize on the measurements made on a few individuals the population as a whole. Modern sampling techniques are used to counter the threats to external validity.
- Construct validity: addresses the question whether the indicator used really indicates what it is supposed to. This question has been discussed in Chapter IV on the specification of project objectives, and more generally in the Chapter III on social indicators in Part II, Section 2.
- Measurement reliability: addresses the question of careful data collection in the field and of rigorous data processing.
- Policy validity: the policy validity depends on the sensitivity of decision-makers to variations in the measurements. It has been discussed earlier (see Part III, Chapter VI, Section 2).

Evaluation designs

The different types of data collection designs will be analysed according to their costs and their ability to distinguish the effects of the project from other possible changes that might not be related to the project activities.

i) Case study with one measurement and no control group

The measurements are limited to the treatment population and are taken only once at some point in time after the activities have been administered. The actual project performance is then compared with the planned performance. A comparison is obviously only meaningful if:
- the goals have been expressed in measurable terms;
- the goals are appropriate and realistic.

This is by far the cheapest, although unfortunately the weakest, evaluation design. The problems of such a design are obvious:
- Since there are no base line data (before the project measurement) available, we are not sure that the effects have occurred since project implementation or how much of the effect could have already been measured before.

---

1. Campbell and Stanley: Experimental and Quasi-Experimental Designs of Research, 1966, as cited in P. Rossi and Sonia Wright, op. cit., p. 19.

- Even if the effects have occurred since implementation of the project, we have no way of knowing whether the effects are due to project activities. With such a design, the number of possible competing explanations is nearly unlimited (history, maturation, other projects, etc.).
- With this simplest form of the case study design, therefore, it is difficult, if not impossible, to know if any change has occurred or to assess the degree to which the occurred change can be attributed to the project. The design has therefore to be considered as unsatisfactory and has to be avoided if ever possible.

ii) Case study design with two measurements and no control group

This design consists of two measurements, one before and one after project implementation. This design permits the determination of whether positive change has occurred or not as the before and after measurements can be compared. The design considers the measurement before the programme as the best available estimate of what the values would have been without the programme. The natural limitation of the design is that it cannot control for other factors that might have brought about the observed change. This design is only justified if it is supplemented by an intensive qualitative analysis of the events and if the qualitative analysis permits the eviction of plausible, alternative explanations for the measured changes. This design is most adaptable to the process evaluation exercise. Although the results from a single case study can not be readily generalised to other programmes, they can provide insight that will help the programme improve its operations."[1]
The major problems of the before and after design are:
- the data may reflect short-term fluctuations rather than programme-related changes;
- the after measurement might not capture all the long-term effects;
- the changes might be due to fluctuation or history and might have occurred even without the project;
- other interventions not related to the project might have caused the changes.

iii) Time series design

This design permits the identification of an underlying trend over a period of time and statistical projections of what the situation would have been without the programme. This design obtains data at several points prior to the programme and after its implementation. Statistical methods permit the estimation of the amount of changes due to natural

---

1.   Carol H. Weiss, op. cit., p. 75.

trends and maturation process. The comparison between the actual and projected estimates permit the identification of the net results from the programme. Several measurements after the implementation of the project will assure that the observed changes are stable over time and thus affect long-term trends. The time series design protects against most threats to validity. The changes might, however, always be due to history or to some special event that came along at the same time as the programme. A critical analysis of other plausible explanations has to be done.

The cost of time series designs are greater than the cost of the designs mentioned earlier: time series design requires some technical expertise to undertake statistical projections and requires data collection at several points in time. Time series designs are only feasible if data over several years before the project have been collected. It is necessary to be very careful in determining whether the data collected for prior years are compatible with the data collected since project implementation.

iv) The introduction of a control group into the evaluation design

Evaluation designs which use for comparison a control group, collect measurements not only on the target population, but also on a non-treated group which is supposed to have similar characteristics to the target population:

a) Case study design with one measurement and a comparison group. The simple case study design (see design no. 1 above) can be improved by adding a comparison group which is similar to the programme population. If the control group shows the same changes as the programme group, it is probable that the changes are not due to the programme. However, if the effects differ between the control and programme group, the net difference may be attributed to the project. The value of the method obviously depends on the similarity of the target group and the control group. The limitation of the design to one measurement after project implementation does not allow to determine whether the control and programme group have not shown the same differences before the project was implemented.

The design is a relatively cheap and simple one. However, it is also one of the weakest evaluation designs. The design should only be used if we have strong circumstantial evidence that the difference in the measured effects is related to the project.

b) Evaluation designs with several measurements and a control group. These evaluations can be divided into two groups:
   - quasi experimental designs;
   - experimental designs.

v)   Quasi experimental designs

Quasi experimental designs involve two or more measurements
in time on a control group and the treatment or experimental group.
Data are collected on both the control and treatment group before and
after the implementation of the project.   The changes in the values
are then compared and both rates of change as well as amount of change
between the two groups compared.   This design protects against changes
that might have occurred from other factors that are concurrent with
the project execution.   The major difficulty of the design is to assure
that the control and experimental group have similar characteristics.
Since the programmes normally depend on voluntary participation, it
is dangerous to compare the participants of a programme with the non-
participants as they are likely to have different motivations and personal
characteristics.   There are several statistical methods available to
match non-equivalent control groups (matching procedures, multi-
variate analysis, etc.).   However, the disagreement on the usefulness
of those methods and the high degree of skill levels required prohibit
their use in everyday evaluations.   Rigorous quasi experimental designs,
coupled with a thorough attempt to identify other plausible explanations,
probably give the highest level of confidence that can be attained in
everyday evaluation.   The cost of quasi experimental designs obviously
varies with the number of measurements taken and the effort made
to assure that the control group is as similar as possible to the treatment group.   The cost includes:
- statistical competence for the collection and, in particular
  the analysis of the data;
- the identification of a comparable control group;
- the collection of comparable data for both the treatment group
  and the control group.

vi)   The experimental design

This is the most powerful but also most difficult and most costly
design.   "It assesses the effectiveness of a programme by systematically comparing specific changes in two or more carefully separated
groups: ones in which the programme is operating and others in which
it is not. "[1] The difference between quasi experimental and experimental
designs lies in the way the control and treatment groups are chosen:
the experimental design assigns the target population randomly either
to the treatment group or to the control group.   Random assignment
means that every member of the target population has an equal chance
of being selected for either the control or the treatment group.
Random assignment assures that the control and treatment are as
similar as possible.   The experimental designs "exceptional ability

---

1.   Harry P. Harty, op. cit., p. 56.

to rule out competing explanations for effects makes the randomised controlled experiment so attractive as a research design".[1] Since the two groups initially differ only through the operation of chance factors, there are only two possible explanations for differences in the effects between the two groups after the treatment has taken place: chance factors in randomisation that produce initial differences or the effects of the treatment. Since differences due to the chance factors have known properties, they can be ruled out through statistical inferences.

It is rare that experimental designs can be used to evaluate Government programmes:

- It is mostly not possible to choose the participants of a programme in a randomised way (practical, moral and political constraints).
- The design requires highly qualified personnel.
- A considerable amount of time is required to plan the design, to collect the information and to analyse the data collected.

Despite the fact that the controlled experimentation is by far the most powerful evaluation design, it does not provide control for all alternative explanations. It is thus still necessary to look for plausible explanations for differences between the two groups.

Thus experimental designs can only be used very rarely in evaluation. They are adapted to one type of evaluation: the evaluation research.

The different evaluation designs discussed in this section and their characteristics are summarised in Figure XVI.

The choice of an evaluation design

The choice of an evaluation design depends on:
- the use that will be made of the evaluation results;
- the type of evaluation chosen;
- the time, money and skills available.

Very often the evaluator does not have the choice among all the alternative designs described above: field conditions will almost always impose severe limits on the kinds of studies which can be successfully carried to completion. Thus the choice of an evaluation design will depend on the purpose of the evaluation and on the resources available. The following factors will have to be taken into account:

- the evaluation design chosen will depend on our ability to exclude alternative, plausible explanations for the observed change by circumstantial evidence. For example, the comparative evaluation of the same programme in different environments will provide relatively strong circumstantial evidence about which effects of the project can be attributed to the project itself and which are dependent on the environment;

---

1. Peter H. Rossi, Sonia R. Wright, op. cit., p. 15.

Figure XVI. DATA COLLECTION DESIGNS AND THEIR CHARACTERISTICS

CHARACTERISTICS / EVALUATION DESIGN	COST	RELIABILITY	TECHNICAL EXPERTISE	TYPE OF EVALUATION PRIMARILY ADAPTED TO THE DESIGN	ABILITY TO MEASURE WHAT IS HAPPENING	ABILITY TO EXCLUDE RIVAL HYPOTHESES
Case study: one measurement	Low	Very low	Low	Reporting	Very low	Non-existant
Case study: two measurements	Medium	Low	Low	Process evaluation	Good	Low
Time series design	Relatively low, if feasible	Medium	Medium	Impact evaluation	Very good	Medium
Case study with one measurement and a control group	Medium	Low	Low	Formative evaluation	Low	Low
Quasi-experimental design	Relatively high (variable)	Relatively high (variable)	Relatively high	Impact evaluation	Very good	Good (variable)
Experimental design	Expensive			Evaluation research	Very good	Very good

- the evaluation design depends on our understanding of the project: formative evaluation of a relatively new project will rely on simple evaluation designs and circumstantial evidence to refine the project understanding. It is only once the project mechanisms are relatively well understood that more powerful evaluation designs become interesting.

An administrator choosing among alternative evaluation designs should follow two principles:[1]

- be realistic about the resources and constraints. It is better to have a simple study whose requirements can be met than to have a more sophisticated design whose requirements must be compromised in the course of gathering field data;
- use the best talent available to verify the study plans. It is better to know the limitations of the design before heavy investment in field data gathering than not to know them at all or to know them only after the investment has bee made.

The progression from a relatively unstructured action to a well-defined policy and the associated evaluation designs are depicted in Figure XVII.

4. Data Collection, Processing and Presentation[2]

Once we have determined the minimum of information required and the monitoring/evaluation design, it is necessary to determine how to collect the information in the field.

1. Data collection[3]

There are basically four means available for data collection:

a) The use of existing statistics: The various Government services collect periodically statistics which can be used for monitoring/evaluation purposes. However, it is rare that those statistics are sufficient. In certain cases those records can be used as a substitute for a control group in time series designs. If used, Government statistics have to be checked for their consistency: an increase in a crime rate might be due to a redefinition of what constitutes a crime; an increase in the number of sicknesses to better record keeping, etc.

b) The use of project reports: An expanded accounting and management monitoring system permits information to be obtained on

---

1. Office of Nutrition, USAID, op. cit., p. 19.

2. This section contains only a review of the basic principles of data collection and processing. The problems of data collection and processing are dealt with in detail in "Doing Evaluation: A Handbook of Procedures", to be published by the OECD Development Centre in early 1978.

3. For the necessary characteristics of data, see Part II, Chapter III, Section 3.

Figure XVII. POLICY DEVELOPMENT AND EVALUATION DESIGNS

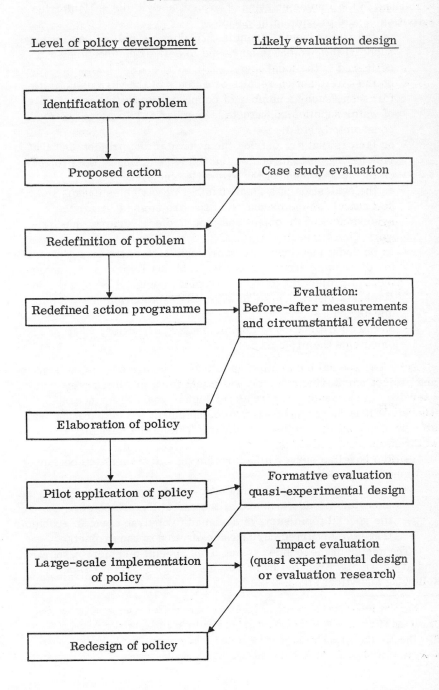

Level of policy development   Likely evaluation design

| Identification of problem |

| Proposed action | → | Case study evaluation |

| Redefinition of problem |

| Redefined action programme | → | Evaluation: Before-after measurements and circumstantial evidence |

| Elaboration of policy |

| Pilot application of policy | → | Formative evaluation quasi-experimental design |

| Large-scale implementation of policy | → | Impact evaluation (quasi experimental design or evaluation research) |

| Redesign of policy |

inputs, outputs and some purposes.[1] Standard reporting systems have
to be established for each activity and by each agent to determine
variations in the implementation of project activities.[2] Monitoring
activities should provide information:

- on the major inputs (financial, training, supplies, institutional
  support) the project is supposed to deliver and how they are
  delivered at the local level;
- on the direct action results or outputs of the various activities
  foreseen, such as number of people treated/sickness; number
  of water supplies constructed; number of kilometres of roads
  constructed, etc.);
- on factors that are outside the control of the project, but that
  risk having an influence on the implementation of the project or
  on the achievement of the project's objectives;
- on the evaluation of a small number of variables considered to
  be critical for the execution of the project and/or for the
  achievement of its objectives (see Project Performance Network Chart above);
- on periodic meetings with representatives of the target population
  for discussing experiences and problems related to the achievement of project objectives. Properly designed reporting and
  synthesis instruments will allow the exploitation of such informal
  discussions;
- on the co-ordination of complementary activities, whether inside
  or outside the project.

c) The special data collection effort: The use of existing statistics
and project monitoring is rarely sufficient for a monitoring/evaluation
exercise, in particular insofar as the higher goals are concerned.
Therefore it is mostly necessary to complement the information available by a special data collection effort. This effort normally consists
of three discrete activities:

- the baseline survey to determine the situation at the beginning
  of the project;
- the resurveys of the communities of the baseline study, normally
  executed at mid-term and at the end of the project;
- the special topic surveys designed to analyse specific problems
  that have occurred during the execution of the project.

The design of these surveys requires special technical resources
and are normally executed by an outside agency. Surveys require the
following analytical steps:

---

1. Not all purposes (and even less the goals) can be monitored as the time lag between
output and effects is too long to be captured in a periodic data collection system.

2. The reporting system has to be tailor made for the project. Standardisation, however, is required for all the reports within the project to allow aggregation and comparison.

i) Determination of the unit to be investigated

According to the purpose of the survey, the unit for the basic data set will change, e.g., the individual, the household, farm unit, community, village, etc.

ii) Determination of the number of units to be investigated, i.e. the sample size

The sample size depends on:
- the variation within the population, but of course this is usually unknown;
- methodological considerations (sample technique);
- resources available;
- confidence required;
- the number of sub-groups considered.

The following factors should be considered:
- the sample size depends on our knowledge about the population. A good stratification of a population allows one to account for a large part of the variation among the units in advance by the strata chosen;[1]
- the absolute number in a sample is the dominant factor and not the sample size relative to the population;[2]
- as a rule of thumb any sub-group should include at least 20 units.[3] Since drop-outs in a sample are often frequent, it is necessary to increase by 10-15 percent the minimum number required in the sample.

iii) Design of the questionnaire

The questionnaires are necessary when the data cannot be collected by direct observation, i.e., for most of the behavioural and nearly all attitudinal questions. The drafting of a questionnaire is a delicate matter, and there are very few operational rules that can be used to assure that the questions are unambiguous and unbiased.[4] Careful pre-testing is necessary for each questionnaire.

---

1. For considerations to be taken into account in the identification of strata, see UN Secretariat: Systematic Monitoring and Evaluation of Integrated Development Programmes (see selected references), pp. 73-81.

2. For sampling errors, see Weiss and Hatry: An Introduction to Sample Surveys for Government Managers, (see selected references), pp. 25-29.

3. USAID: "Field Guide for Evaluation in Nutrition Education", p. 27 (see selected references).

4. Questions often provide cues to the respondant. "Many people actually tend to give 'acceptable' or 'expected' answers, responding to these cues by tailoring their answers to fit the situation as they perceive it", (Hatry, Weiss, op. cit., p. 50). This is particularly true if the interviewers are perceived, rightly or wrongly, as part of the Government.

iv)   Selection and training of interviewers

The relation the interviewer establishes with the respondant is one of the most important imponderables affecting the accuracy of survey data.   Careful selection, training and retraining of the interviewers is therefore very important.   Random checks on interviews during the implementation of the questionnaire is probably the most important factor to assure the accuracy of the data collected. It is important to remember that in less developed countries, the most important source of inaccuracies in data are due to faulty data collection and processing, and not to sampling errors.

d)   Ratings by experts: Not all information can be measured. Especially in the social fields, an attempt to quantify the unquantifiable may lead to absurd results (e. g. , the value of human life expressed in terms of the cost of bringing up a person or in terms of the value of the production lost).   Various rating procedures may allow the expression of expert judgments in a comparable way.   The accuracy of a rating system depends on the quality of the investigators chosen, and on the discretion power provided by the chosen scale.   Scales have to be pre-tested to determine the confidence level one can put into their results.

2.   Data processing and analysis

Data processing is a time-consuming exercise requiring special skills and a high level of technical rigour.   Data processing is very often the stumbling block of monitoring/evaluation frameworks.   It is not infrequent that large numbers of data are never processed and mostly only a fraction of the data can be analysed in time for the decision-making process.   To avoid waste of resources, a critical assessment of the capability to process and analyse the data within the time required for their use in decision-making should provide the major criterion for the amount of information to be collected.

The complexity of the task is determined by the type of analysis chosen.   Since technical expertise and time are in short supply in monitoring/evaluation exercises "... common sense and logical reasoning should replace statistical manipulation as the main tool of analysis".[1]   The logical structure of the project will provide the necessary framework for the tabulation (and cross-tabulations) of variables.

3.   The presentation of monitoring/evaluation results

The form and content of evaluation results have to correspond to the needs and capabilities of the users of the monitoring/evaluation system.   The following principles should be taken into account in drafting the evaluation report.

---

1.   UN Secretariat "Systematic Monitoring and Evaluation of Integrated Development Programmes", op. cit., p. 125.

- the evaluation report should be action oriented: Often evaluation reports go into great length describing the situation and identifying shortcomings without proposing actions that could or should be taken;
- the evaluation report should be understandable to the layman. Often evaluation reports are rather academic and burdened with methodological questions. It is necessary to streamline an evaluation report providing general conclusions and actions proposed. Supporting statistical material needs to be annexed;
- the evaluation report should also reflect management's position. Before the dissemination, the report has to be discussed with the various management levels concerned. The discussion should lead to a concensus on the situation of the project and on the proposed actions. Management, which is supposed to act upon the evaluation report will only do so if they have been convinced of the analysis proposed;
- the evaluation report should address each specific management level involved. Monitoring/evaluation information can only lead to action if resources and procedures exist to respond to the information and if management responsibilities are not too diffuse and numerous. Monitoring/evaluation information thus has a greater chance of being acted upon:
  - if it is addressed to specific management levels;
  - if the recommendations take into account the resources and procedures at the disposition of each management level;
  - if a follow-up is foreseen to determine the actions taken on the information.

4.   Testing the utilisation of a monitoring/evaluation system

Like any other project activity, the monitoring/evaluation system will have to be checked in terms of its usefulness.

The goal of the monitoring/evaluation system is to contribute to the achievement of project and/or policy objectives.

It will mostly be rather difficult to prove the contribution of the monitoring/evaluation system to the achievement of the project's or policies' objectives in an objective way, as there exists normally no comparison group. However, the analysis of the decisions taken and a trend analysis of their results often provides quite strong circumstantial evidence about the effectiveness of a monitoring/evaluation system. The critical steps that lead to the objective and that can easily be monitored are:
- information gathered in a cost-effective way and with adequate technical rigour;
- does the information reach the various decision-makers in time;
- what are the decisions taken upon the information provided by the monitoring/evaluation system;
- what actions have followed those decisions.

The design of a monitoring/evaluation system is not a one time shot. Its periodic assessment permits the abandoning of information that is not used and to collect new information according to the evolution of the activities.

VII

INSTITUTIONAL ASPECTS OF
MONITORING/EVALUATION

1. The·importance of high-level commitment to evaluation

This commitment is essential to create an evaluative spirit. It is
certain that a monitoring/evaluation framework constitutes a source
of threat and possible annoyance to project management. It requires
an additional effort in management with uncertain benefits. Project
management thus will only collaborate actively if the monitoring/eval-
uation system has high-level support.

2. Responsibilities of project management

To assure the usefulness of a monitoring/evaluation system, it is
necessary that project management be held responsible not only for the
delivery of services and outputs, but for the achievement of objectives.
Project management is every day confronted by a number of urgent
operational problems. It is therefore natural that in an action setting,
monitoring/evaluation tasks get low priority. If project management is
not persuaded that it is effects and not outputs that count in the eyes of
the agency's management, they will resent and passively boycott a
monitoring/evaluation system. It is therefore necessary that the
rewarding system in an agency be based on the manager's effectiveness
in achieving objectives rather than his efficiency in providing services
or producing products.

3. The evaluation unit

Since management invariable gets absorbed by daily operational
tasks, it is necessary that evaluation tasks be executed by a specific
person who is removed from daily operational responsibilities. Diffuse
responsibilities for evaluation are hardly ever effective. The creation of a
monitoring/evaluation unit at the agency and project level[1] requires the
solution of the two following problems:

---

1. Such units will obviously only be created for those projects that have been selected for
a monitoring/evaluation exercise (see Chapter V, Part III).

- The place of the evaluation unit in the management structure

The monitoring/evaluation unit should be close to the decision-making level which uses its information. Since a monitoring/evaluation unit intervenes in all activities of the project and at various levels, it is necessary that it has the authority of a relatively high management level. However, it is important that the evaluation unit is within and not outside the management structure. To assure that the unit is responsive to the problems of project or policy execution and that the information generated is used, it is necessary that the unit is clearly integrated into the project or the agency. An independent unit risks to follow its own logic and purpose and its results are sure to be rejected by project or policy management. The objectivity of the results of the monitoring/evaluation exercise will have to be assured by other mechanisms (see below).

- The relation between evaluators and operational management

The relation between evaluators and operational personnel of the project is not an easy one. Operational personnel have a tendency to consider evaluators as parias who are paid to observe and who do not need to dirty their hands with daily problems. On the other hand, evaluators often have a tendency to consider themselves as inspectors and not to be sensitive enough to the problems of the operational side of the project. However, the success of the monitoring/evaluation exercise and its usefulness to project management depend to a large extent on the dialogue between operational management and evaluators. Evaluators have to spell out the problems of project management. They have to explain to project management the purpose of their activities and how to use the information for management decisions. Often management does not make full use of the monitoring/evaluation unit as they do not know what services this unit can provide nor how to integrate the information created into their decision-making process. To have a fruitful dialogue - a pre-condition for a useful monitoring/evaluation system - it is necessary that both parties have a good knowledge of the other's activities and problems and that they are sensitive to the constraints under which each one of them is working.

4. At what moment should a monitoring/evaluation system be set up?

As indicated earlier, a monitoring/evaluation system has to be designed at the very beginning of the project. There are three specific points in time at which the monitoring evaluation system could be set up:

- during the appraisal mission. Since the evaluation design is closely related to the project design, the appraisal mission seems to be the ideal moment to set up a monitoring/evaluation system. However, there are some serious short-comings to such an approach:

- in an appraisal mission the team is very concerned with identifying actions that could be executed. The thrust of the appraisal mission consists of comparing alternative actions rather than defining the logic of the actions proposed. At that stage, problems of monitoring/evaluation have a very low priority, and a serious consideration of the project's logic is premature;
- in an appraisal mission, project components and their potential effects are identified. However, they are not yet worked out in detail. The monitoring/evaluation design requires a detailed analysis of the various components of the project, which will only be forthcoming later on;
- The general management organigram provided by an appraisal mission is not sufficient for the design of a monitoring/evaluation system. To identify the users of the information, their needs and their capacity to use or generate information, the designer of an evaluation system needs a detailed organisational structure of the project, including job descriptions, lines of responsibilities and the qualifications required for each job.

- at the project approval stage. The setting up of a monitoring/evaluation system at the project approval stage has the following advantages:
    - the project components and the project's logic are clearly identified;
    - the management structure of the project is available;
    - the baseline survey can be planned and executed before the project starts.

However, there is a serious disadvantage: the absence of a meaningful dialogue. The appraisors consider their job as finished and the project implementation team is not yet constituted. The monitoring/evaluation designer risks to work in a vacuum.

- at the beginning of the implementation stage. The advantages are the following:
    - a dialogue is possible with project management;
    - the users of the information and their capabilities can be assessed;
    - the users of the monitoring/evaluation system can participate in its design.

The disadvantage results from the problems related to the starting of a new project and the unavailability of project management to discuss monitoring/evaluation issues. The design of the monitoring/evaluation system risks being postponed and baseline data and monitoring activities cannot be implemented in time.

Using the terminology employed in Figure XVI, the following timing is suggested:

162

- appraisal/approval stage: Design of the feasible model for project monitoring/evaluation and of the baseline survey;
- implementation stage: Design of the practical model for project monitoring/evaluation.

5. Who should execute the monitoring/evaluation system?

The question of who should be entrusted with the monitoring/ evaluation tasks is guided by the following two principles:
- to assure the credibility of an evaluation, the staff who operates a programme or project should not be responsible for its evaluation;
- the active participation of the operational staff in the monitoring/ evaluation exercise is necessary for the following reasons:
  - their collaboration is required to gain access to the information;
  - their collaboration is required to act upon the information gathered;
  - monitoring/evaluation is an integral part of management tasks.
Therefore a combination of outside investigations and in-house monitoring is necessary:
- The monitoring tasks should be executed within the agency: Monitoring activities can best be executed by project or programme staff. They have access to the information and no special skills are needed to collect the information. Central staff should supervise and control the implementation of the monitoring system by the various agents involved.
- The survey tasks should be executed by outside consultants: The baseline survey, the re-study and special topic surveys require special skills and a high level of technical rigour not normally available within a project or an agency. Moreover, the surveys address primarily the question of effects and the achievement of higher objectives by the project, domains in which the credibility of an evaluation is much more difficult to judge. Thus the outside involvement for the surveys will fulfill two objectives:
  - assure the technical rigour of the surveys;
  - assure the objectivity and credibility of the results.

VIII

RESUME AND CONCLUSIONS

1.   The discussion of monitoring/evaluation frameworks is based on the following considerations:

- Traditional reporting and evaluation practices are not adapted to the information needs of an efficient management of development activities.

- Experience shows that information generated by evaluations is rarely used in the decision-making process and that most evaluation results are dismissed as irrelevant to real issues and concerns.

- Monitoring/evaluation is the art of the possible: evaluation frameworks have to strike a compromise between technical rigour, resources available and the timeliness of the information.

- There exists no general monitoring/evaluation framework. Each project and programme has its own information requirements, its own management structure and its specific resource constraints. Monitoring/evaluation frameworks thus have to be tailor made.

2.   The proposed approach is based on the following concepts:

- The evaluator is at the mercy of the project or programme design. A clearly articulated programme is a pre-condition for a useful evaluation. It is therefore necessary that the evaluator be involved from the very beginning of the project.

- More questions are asked from the evaluator than he can answer. It is necessary for the evaluator to make an evaluability assessment of the programme and to come to an agreement with the users on the questions he can find answers to.

- Evaluation requests as much from the sponsor as it does from the evaluator. There has to be improved communication between the evaluator and the users of evaluations. The following points have to be clarified before an evaluation is undertaken:
  - measures of success are not well defined. The dialogue between user and evaluator has to define and establish agreement on those measures of success;

164

- conclusive evidence is a matter of judgement. Therefore it is necessary to establish "agreed-on standards of success", i. e. it has to be determined what kind of evidence would be conclusive enough to warrant a policy decision;
- the use (and users) of the evaluation results has to be defined before the evaluation is undertaken. It is necessary to show the practical influence of evaluation on the management of the development activities.

3. The proposed approach attempts to assure the usefulness of monitoring/evaluation activities by determining:
- who needs what information when?
- how important is the information for the decision-making process?
- how can the required information be expressed in measurable terms?
- what sort of data can be collected, given the human and financial resource constraints?
- what type of evaluation and which evaluation design can generate the information required in the most cost-effective way?
- how to collect, process and present the data.

IX

SELECTED ANNOTATED REFERENCES

A. GENERAL REFERENCE WORKS ON EVALUATION RESEARCH IN SOCIAL SCIENCES

United Nations, Department of Economic and Social Affairs:

Monitoring and Evaluation Systems for Assessing Developmental Impact at the Local Level: An Annotated Bibliography, prepared by the United Nations Secretariat, 11th October 1976, New York.

The bibliography contains references to the social science literature on systematic project evaluation. It contains 169 entries, most of them annotated. The entries are by author, and a key word index aids the reader in locating titles of particular interest.

The following three entries provide an overview of the problems in the evaluation of social programmes:

Peter Rossi and Walter Williams (eds.)

Evaluating Social Programs: Theory, Practice and Politics, New York, Seminar Press, 1972, 326 pages.

Francis G. Caro (ed.)

Reading in Evaluation Research , 3rd edition, N.Y. Russell Sage Foundation, 1975, 418 pages.

Elmer L. Struening and Marcia Guttentag (eds.)

Handbook of Evaluation Research, Beverly Hills–London, Sage, 1975; 2 volumes (Vol. 1: 704 pages; Vol. 2: 744 pages).

B. SPECIAL TOPICS IN EVALUATION RESEARCH

Caroll H. Weiss

Evaluation Research: Methods of Assessing Program Effectiveness Prentice Hall, Methods of Social Science Series, Englewoods Cliffs, New Jersey, 1972.

This book, designed as a basic text in courses on evaluation research discusses the principles of evaluation research in a non-technical language. The publication discusses the purpose of evaluation, the formulation of programme goals in measurable terms and describes the various evaluation designs. Problems in the creation of a research programme attached to an action programme are discussed in a realistic manner. The author discusses means to improve the utilisation of evaluation results.

Peter H. Rossi and Sonia R. Wright

Evaluation Research: An Assessment of Current Theory and Politics, UNESCO unpublished paper, Paris, September 1976.

The paper discusses the distinctive features of evaluation research, and its major problems. Four critical issues in evaluation research are identified. The art of evaluation is "to make do with considerably less than one would ideally desire". The authors discuss the different data collection designs and distinguish the various evaluation designs illustrated from US experiences with evaluation.

Howard E. Freeman

The Present Status of Evaluation Research, UNESCO, unpublished working paper, Paris, August 1976.

The author stresses the dual pressures of methodology rigour and policy utility in evaluation designs. The boundaries of evaluation research are given and the author defines evaluation as "activities which follow general mandates of social science research . . . ". The present status of process and impact evaluation is discussed and the author concludes with a plea ". . . to address political and contextual problems that inhibit successful completion and utilisation of evaluation research".

Ilene Nagel Bernstein

Evaluation Research: Development and Dissemination of Evaluation Techniques, UNESCO, unpublished paper, Paris, September 1976.

The author draws the following conclusions from evaluation experiences: 1) evaluation research efforts have failed to live up to their promises; 2) few evaluations use prescribed methodology; 3) the results are not disseminated. To remedy the situation the author proposes a centralisation and connection of policy power to policy research and implementation. The author considers that the design of intervention programmes should be fitted to the methodological needs of a rigorous evaluation and better monitoring activities.

Carol H. Weiss

"Evaluation Research in the Political Context", in Handbook of Evaluation Research, Vol. 1, op. cit. , p. 13-26.

The article discusses the political implications of evaluation research. Political considerations intrude in three major ways into evaluation:
- policies and programmes, i. e. the objects of an evaluation exercise, are political decisions;
- evaluation reports, i. e. the output of the evaluation exercise, enter the political arena;
- evaluation itself, i. e. its content, has a political nature.

Because of these political implications the author considers that there exist more fruitful ways for a social scientist than evaluation research.

Donald T. Campbell

"Reforms as Experiments", in Handbook of Evaluation Research, pp. 71-100.

The author discusses the different threats to validity of evaluation results and discusses the limits and merits of various evaluation designs.

Jum C. Numally, Williams H. Wilson

"Method and Theory for Developing Measures in Evaluation Research", in Handbook of Evaluation Research, op. cit. , pp. 227-288.

The author discusses the reasons for standardised measures and the different scales in use. A discussion of scaling of psychological attributes leads to the treatment of various scaling models for people. A special chapter is devoted to the construction of lists (achievement lists, criterion approach and speed lists).

C. MORE PRACTICAL GUIDES ON HOW TO SET UP AND EXECUTE EVALUATION

Peter Rossi et al.

Doing Evaluation: A Handbook of Procedures, OECD Development Centre, to be published early 1978.

The handbook, addressed to the practioners in the field, provides the necessary technical information to execute evaluations in the social fields. The first volume describes procedures requiring minimal resources and the second volume more complex designs and analyses.

All the concepts and techniques are discussed on the basis of real world examples. The volumes provide technical notes in the annexes and an annotated guide to the relevant literature.

Harry P. Hatry, Richard E. Wimie, Donald M. Frisk

Practical Programme Evaluation for State and Local Government Officials, The Urban Institute, Washington, 1973.

This publication discusses the scope and current practices in evaluation. The authors insist on the specification exercise and consider comparison as the basis of all evaluations. Different data collection designs are discussed in terms of their utility for policy decisions. Various data collection methods are discussed and their limitations identified. The concepts are illustrated by a case study, "a special city clean-up operation". A special chapter is devoted to institutional issues and the authors conclude that "evaluation as a management tool, must, in the end, demonstrate its worth in leading to reduced costs or improved effectiveness of Government programmes" (126).

John D. Waller et al.

Monitoring for Government Agencies, The Urban Institute, Washington, February 1976.

This publication discusses in the form of a practical handbook the role of monitoring in Government Agencies and the major monitoring problems. Four major monitoring tasks are outlined: 1) establish agreement with uses of monitoring system on information required; 2) establish agreement with project personnel on what will be monitored; 3) establish the information flow; and 4) assure the utilisation of monitoring information. Each step is analysed in terms of its meanings and practical guides are given to assure its implementation. The publication has the merit of not only saying what to do, but suggesting practical steps on how to do it in different administrative set-ups. An appendix provides examples of procedures and materials used in monitoring, based on US Government programmes.

Joseph S. Wholey

A Methodology for Planning and Conducting Project Impact Evaluations in UNESCO Fields, UNESCO, Paris, unpublished paper, 1976.

The author defines evaluation as "measurements and comparisons to provide specific information on projects' results for use in specific policy and management decisions". The author insists on the policy usefulness of evaluation studies. Clarification of objectives and the dialogue with the intended users is stressed. The author proposes for impact evaluation a comparison between actual versus expected performance. Stress is laid upon the dissemination of the results in policy relevant formats.

Joseph S. Wholey, Joe N. Nay et al.

"Evaluation: When is it really needed?", in Evaluation Magazine, Vol. 2, No. 2 (1975), pp. 89-93.

The criticism of current evaluation practices is based on technical and utility criteria. The author proposes an alternative approach stressing the evaluability assessment, the significance of the evaluation and rapid feedbacks for policy makers. The author considers that performance monitoring is often the most cost-effective evaluation that can be obtained under real-world conditions.

Pamela Horst, Joe N. Nay et al.

"Programme Management and the Federal Evaluation", in Public Administration Review, July/August 1974, pp. 306 et seq.

Three reasons are given for the failure of evaluations to lead to more effective social policies or programmes: 1) lack of definitions; 2) lack of clear logic of testable assumptions; 3) lack of management. The author concludes that evaluation can only be more effective if greater leverage can be applied to administrations for effective delivery of public services. Evaluation design is considered as an analytical exercise to explicit the project design.

Caroll H. Weiss and Harry P. Hatry

An Introduction to Sample Surveys for Government Managers, The Urban Institute, March 1971.

This is a non-technical paper for managers providing some perspective on the nature and implications of sample surveys, their likely costs, and what can be expected from them. The paper discusses the survey process, characteristics and costs. The problem of accuracy, and the various sources of error are discussed. The trade-offs between costs and accuracy are treated.

D. MONITORING/EVALUATION IN SPECIFIC FIELDS

Guido J. Deboeck

Monitoring and Evaluation of Agricultural and Rural Development Projects: Basic Concepts, Design and Illustration, World Bank, 15th July, 1976 (unpublished), ROR Support Unit.

This paper discusses the various types of monitoring and evaluation and discusses the principles of a monitoring/evaluation design. The methodology for information collection and analysis is based on the logical framework. The concepts are illustrated by six case studies.

United Nations, Department of Economic and Social Affairs

Systematic Monitoring and Evaluation of Integrated Development Programmes, Social Development Division, Institutional Development and Popular Participation Section, New York, April 1976.

This paper consists of two parts: Part I provides a general overview of concepts of systematic monitoring and evaluation outlining the critical issues in setting up an information system. The second part discusses four field applications. The paper provides a practical guide to the design and implementation of baseline studies consisting of the following steps: 1) determination of what to measure; 2) determination of number of case studies; 3) sample of case studies; 4) determining number of individuals per community; 5) designing the questionnaire; 6) field work and pretabulation of data; 7) data analysis. Special chapters are devoted to the execution of re-studies of communities and to the special case of monitoring and evaluation of training inputs.

Augustin Lombana Marino

Evaluation of a Rural Development Project in Colombia: Critical Analysis with Methodological Conclusions, UNESCO, unpublished paper, Paris, September 1976.

This paper analyses the experience in evaluating "Rural Development Concentrations Project in Colombia". The author analyses the project objectives, the hypotheses on which they are based. The paper provides an analysis of the planned phases and includes a critique of the project design. The author proposes a permanent evaluation outline executed by a mixed evaluation team including administrators, executive personnel and external evaluators and community participation.

Office of Nutrition, Technical Assistance Bureau

A Field Guide for Evaluation of Nutrition Education: An Experimental Approach to Determination of Effects on Food Behaviour in Lesser Developed Countries, USAID, Washington, June 1975.

The guide is based on the recognition that dietary surveys are too costly and complicated and that most nutrition education evaluation measures knowledge rather than food consumption. The method is based on measurements collected on the basis of a 24-hour recall period for up to 5 measures over a period of 6 to 18 months. The criteria for evaluation are defined by users. The publication discusses the planning and design of an evaluation study, the collection of data, their analysis and the use of the evaluation results.

Office of Nutrition, Technical Assistance Bureau

Application of a Field Guide for Evaluation of Nutrition Education in Three Programmes in Brazil, USAID, Washington, March 1976.

This publication consists of the application of the field guide to three kinds of nutrition education programmes (person-to-person, group teaching, and mass media) in Brazil.

OECD SALES AGENTS
DÉPOSITAIRES DES PUBLICATIONS DE L'OCDE

ARGENTINA – ARGENTINE
Carlos Hirsch S.R.L., Florida 165, 4° Piso (Galería Guemes)
1333 BUENOS AIRES, Tel. 33.1787.2391 y 30.7122

AUSTRALIA – AUSTRALIE
Australia and New Zealand Book Company Pty, Ltd.,
10 Aquatic Drive, Frenchs Forest, N.S.W. 2086
P.O. Box 459, BROOKVALE, N.S.W. 2100. Tel. (02) 452.44.11

AUSTRIA – AUTRICHE
OECD Publications and Information Center
4 Simrockstrasse 5300 Bonn (Germany). Tel. (0228) 21.60.45
Local Agent/Agent local :
Gerold and Co., Graben 31, WIEN 1. Tel. 52.22.35

BELGIUM – BELGIQUE
Jean De Lannoy, Service Publications OCDE
avenue du Roi 202, B-1060 BRUXELLES. Tel. 02/538.51.69

CANADA
Renouf Publishing Company Limited,
Central Distribution Centre,
61 Sparks Street (Mall),
P.O.B. 1008 - Station B,
OTTAWA, Ont. KIP 5R1.
Tel. (613)238.8985-6
Toll Free: 1-800.267.4164
Librairie Renouf Limitée
980 rue Notre-Dame,
Lachine, P.Q. H8S 2B9,
Tel. (514) 634-7088.

DENMARK – DANEMARK
Munksgaard Export and Subscription Service
35, Nørre Søgade
DK 1370 KØBENHAVN K. Tel. +45.1.12.85.70

FINLAND – FINLANDE
Akateeminen Kirjakauppa
Keskuskatu 1, 00100 HELSINKI 10. Tel. 65.11.22

FRANCE
Bureau des Publications de l'OCDE,
2 rue André-Pascal, 75775 PARIS CEDEX 16. Tel. (1) 524.81.67
Principal correspondant :
13602 AIX-EN-PROVENCE : Librairie de l'Université.
Tel. 26.18.08

GERMANY – ALLEMAGNE
OECD Publications and Information Center
4 Simrockstrasse 5300 BONN Tel. (0228) 21.60.45

GREECE – GRÈCE
Librairie Kauffmann, 28 rue du Stade,
ATHÈNES 132. Tel. 322.21.60

HONG-KONG
Government Information Services,
Publications/Sales Section, Baskerville House,
2nd Floor, 22 Ice House Street

ICELAND – ISLANDE
Snaebjörn Jönsson and Co., h.f.,
Hafnarstraeti 4 and 9, P.O.B. 1131, REYKJAVIK.
Tel. 13133/14281/11936

INDIA – INDE
Oxford Book and Stationery Co. :
NEW DELHI-1, Scindia House. Tel. 45896
CALCUTTA 700016, 17 Park Street. Tel. 240832

INDONESIA – INDONÉSIE
PDIN-LIPI, P.O. Box 3065/JKT., JAKARTA, Tel. 583467

IRELAND – IRLANDE
TDC Publishers – Library Suppliers
12 North Frederick Street, DUBLIN 1 Tel. 744835-749677

ITALY – ITALIE
Libreria Commissionaria Sansoni :
Via Lamarmora 45, 50121 FIRENZE. Tel. 579751/584468
Via Bartolini 29, 20155 MILANO. Tel. 365083
Sub-depositari :
Ugo Tassi
Via A. Farnese 28, 00192 ROMA. Tel. 310590
Editrice e Libreria Herder,
Piazza Montecitorio 120, 00186 ROMA. Tel. 6794628
Costantino Ercolano, Via Generale Orsini 46, 80132 NAPOLI. Tel. 405210
Libreria Hoepli, Via Hoepli 5, 20121 MILANO. Tel. 865446
Libreria Scientifica, Dott. Lucio de Biasio "Aeiou"
Via Meravigli 16, 20123 MILANO Tel. 807679
Libreria Zanichelli
Piazza Galvani 1/A, 40124 Bologna Tel. 237389
Libreria Lattes, Via Garibaldi 3, 10122 TORINO. Tel. 519274
La diffusione delle edizioni OCSE è inoltre assicurata dalle migliori librerie nelle
città più importanti.

JAPAN – JAPON
OECD Publications and Information Center,
Landic Akasaka Bldg., 2-3-4 Akasaka,
Minato-ku, TOKYO 107 Tel. 586.2016

KOREA – CORÉE
Pan Korea Book Corporation,
P.O. Box n° 101 Kwangwhamun, SÉOUL. Tel. 72.7369

LEBANON – LIBAN
Documenta Scientifica/Redico,
Edison Building, Bliss Street, P.O. Box 5641, BEIRUT.
Tel. 354429 – 344425

MALAYSIA – MALAISIE
University of Malaya Co-operative Bookshop Ltd.
P.O. Box 1127, Jalan Pantai Baru
KUALA LUMPUR. Tel. 577701/577072

THE NETHERLANDS – PAYS-BAS
Staatsuitgeverij, Verzendboekhandel,
Chr. Plantijnstraat 1 Postbus 20014
2500 EA S-GRAVENHAGE. Tel. nr. 070.789911
Voor bestellingen: Tel. 070.789208

NEW ZEALAND – NOUVELLE-ZÉLANDE
Publications Section,
Government Printing Office Bookshops:
AUCKLAND: Retail Bookshop: 25 Rutland Street,
Mail Orders: 85 Beach Road, Private Bag C.P.O.
HAMILTON: Retail: Ward Street,
Mail Orders, P.O. Box 857
WELLINGTON: Retail: Mulgrave Street (Head Office),
Cubacade World Trade Centre
Mail Orders: Private Bag
CHRISTCHURCH: Retail: 159 Hereford Street,
Mail Orders: Private Bag
DUNEDIN: Retail: Princes Street
Mail Order: P.O. Box 1104

NORWAY – NORVÈGE
J.G. TANUM A/S
P.O. Box 1177 Sentrum OSLO 1. Tel. (02) 80.12.60

PAKISTAN
Mirza Book Agency, 65 Shahrah Quaid-E-Azam, LAHORE 3.
Tel. 66839

PORTUGAL
Livraria Portugal, Rua do Carmo 70-74,
1117 LISBOA CODEX. Tel. 360582/3

SINGAPORE – SINGAPOUR
Information Publications Pte Ltd,
Pei-Fu Industrial Building,
24 New Industrial Road N° 02-06
SINGAPORE 1953, Tel. 2831786, 2831798

SPAIN – ESPAGNE
Mundi-Prensa Libros, S.A.
Castelló 37, Apartado 1223, MADRID-1. Tel. 275.46.55
Libreria Bosch, Ronda Universidad 11, BARCELONA 7.
Tel. 317.53.08, 317.53.58

SWEDEN – SUÈDE
AB CE Fritzes Kungl Hovbokhandel,
Box 16 356, S 103 27 STH, Regeringsgatan 12,
DS STOCKHOLM. Tel. 08/23.89.00
Subscription Agency/Abonnements:
Wennergren-Williams AB,
Box 13004, S104 25 STOCKHOLM.
Tel. 08/54.12.00

SWITZERLAND – SUISSE
OECD Publications and Information Center
4 Simrockstrasse 5300 BONN (Germany). Tel. (0228) 21.60.45
Local Agents/Agents locaux
Librairie Payot, 6 rue Grenus, 1211 GENÈVE 11. Tel. 022.31.89.50

TAIWAN – FORMOSE
Good Faith Worldwide Int'l Co., Ltd.
9th floor, No. 118, Sec. 2,
Chung Hsiao E. Road
TAIPEI. Tel. 391.7396/391.7397

THAILAND – THAILANDE
Suksit Siam Co., Ltd., 1715 Rama IV Rd,
Samyan, BANGKOK 5. Tel. 2511630

TURKEY – TURQUIE
Kültur Yayinlari Is-Türk Ltd. Sti.
Atatürk Bulvari No : 191/Kat. 21
Kavaklidere/ANKARA. Tel. 17 02 66
Dolmabahce Cad. No : 29
BESIKTAS/ISTANBUL. Tel. 60 71 88

UNITED KINGDOM – ROYAUME-UNI
H.M. Stationery Office,
P.O.B. 276, LONDON SW8 5DT.
(postal orders only)
Telephone orders: (01) 622.3316, or
49 High Holborn, LONDON WCIV 6 HB (personal callers)
Branches at: EDINBURGH, BIRMINGHAM, BRISTOL,
MANCHESTER, BELFAST.

UNITED STATES OF AMERICA – ÉTATS-UNIS
OECD Publications and Information Center, Suite 1207,
1750 Pennsylvania Ave., N.W. WASHINGTON, D.C.20006 – 4582
Tel. (202) 724.1857

VENEZUELA
Libreria del Este, Avda. F. Miranda 52, Edificio Galipan,
CARACAS 106. Tel. 32.23.01/33.26.04/31.58.38

YUGOSLAVIA – YOUGOSLAVIE
Jugoslovenska Knjiga, Knez Mihajlova 2, P.O.B. 36, BEOGRAD.
Tel. 621.992

Les commandes provenant de pays où l'OCDE n'a pas encore désigné de dépositaire peuvent être adressées à :
OCDE, Bureau des Publications, 2, rue André-Pascal, 75775 PARIS CEDEX 16.

Orders and inquiries from countries where sales agents have not yet been appointed may be sent to:
OECD, Publications Office, 2, rue André-Pascal, 75775 PARIS CEDEX 16.

68236-12-1984

OECD PUBLICATIONS
2, rue André-Pascal, 75775 Paris Cedex 16
No. 39.367 1978
PRINTED IN FRANCE